ADVANCE PRAISE FOR

Dear Students

This is the "handbook" I wish had been in my hands as a first-year student at a predominantly white liberal arts college as one of 12 Black students recruited, essentially, to integrate the institution. One parent came from a university-educated family, but she was an immigrant. The other parent finished his high school equivalency in the US Army. Neither were equipped to guide or offer specific help. *Dear Students: 10 Letters to Empower and Transform Your Higher Education Journey* is a volume of "multilingual" letters, so speaks as academic adviser, professor, and parent with concrete how-tos accompanied by institutional, socio-political, and psychological explanations of what students experience often without being able to comprehend fully. Therefore, they fall into the default: self-blame, shame, guilt with not many places to turn. This volume is exactly the resource needed to help ALL students engage fully, take risks, work hard, seek advice and support, and, simply, to bring their whole selves into the higher education institution. Bravo!

—Margo Okazawa-Rey, PhD
Professor Emerita, San Francisco State University

What a gift is this little guidebook! For all the marginalized and disenfranchised students— or any students, in fact—who wonder how to cope with the "hidden curriculum" and their own "imposter syndrome," here are the real answers. Meredith Madden, renowned for connecting with anyone she teaches, tells the secrets of how to "do college." Served up in readable, bite-sized bits of memorable but totally practical wisdom—things you can actually do, things that work—Madden helps students become the masters of their own education while forging the relationships with peers and teachers that can best help them succeed.

—Daniel F. Chambliss, PhD
Eugene M. Tobin Distinguished Professor of Sociology, Emeritus, Hamilton College

Dear Students

Meredith Madden

Dear Students

10 Letters to Empower and Transform Your Higher Education Journey

PETER LANG
Lausanne • Berlin • Bruxelles • Chennai • New York • Oxford

Library of Congress Cataloging-in-Publication Data

Names: Madden, Meredith, 1976- author.
Title: Dear Students: 10 Letters to Empower and Transform Your Higher
Education Journey / Meredith Madden.
Other titles: Ten Letters to Empower and Transform Your Higher Education Journey
Description: First edition. | New York: Peter Lang, [2023] | Includes
bibliographical references.
Identifiers: LCCN 2022060855 (print) | LCCN 2022060856 (ebook) | ISBN
9781433194566 (paperback: alk. paper) | ISBN 9781433194542 (ebook) |
ISBN 9781433194559 (epub)
Subjects: LCSH: First-generation college students—Services for—United
States. | Students with social disabilities—Education (Higher)—United
States. | College student orientation—United States. | College
freshmen—United States. | Educational equalization—United States. |
Educational mobility—United States. | Education, Higher—Social
aspects—United States.
Classification: LCC LC4069.6.M33 2023 (print) | LCC LC4069.6 (ebook) |
DDC 378.1/98—dc23/eng/20230126
LC record available at https://lccn.loc.gov/2022060855
LC ebook record available at https://lccn.loc.gov/2022060856

Bibliographic information published by **Die Deutsche Nationalbibliothek.**
The German National Library lists this publication in the German
National Bibliography; detailed bibliographic data is available
on the Internet at http://dnb.d-nb.de.

Cover design by Peter Lang Group AG

ISBN 9781433194566 (paperback)
ISBN 9781433194542 (ebook)
ISBN 9781433194559 (epub)
DOI 10.3726/b20489

© 2023 Meredith Madden
Published by Peter Lang Publishing Inc., New York, USA
info@peterlang.com - www.peterlang.com

This publication has been peer reviewed.

Dedication

Dedicated with love to:
Ronan Milne
Rachel Madden
Anna Madden
Emerson Eastty
Liam Soden
Alyse Soden
Andres Fluffy Aguilar
Sadé Cardin
Yuri Choi
Sacharja Cunningham
Diamond Jackson
Emily Liu
Sindy Liu
Kelli Mackey
Anna MacDonald
Riley Nichols
Edgar Otero
Shaina Coronel Pazmino
Syon Powell
Joe Pucci
Angélica Ramos
Delta Reyes
Helen Stutsman
Aoífe Thomas
The *Education, Teaching, and Social Change* Class community
My many students past and present on their education journey
who are creating new possibilities for themselves, others, and
their communities
and
Robin Vanderwall

Dr. Margo Okazawa-Rey
Dr. Jack Harris
Dr. Gretchen E. Lopez

CONTENTS

ACKNOWLEDGMENTS

For me writing has always been an expression of love. This book is anchored in a history of love and connection to so many people who have walked alongside me over the many moments of my life's journey. The idea for this book came as I finished a three-year teaching contract in the Education Studies program at Hamilton College. While I had been an adjunct professor for six years during graduate school, the position at Hamilton was my first full-time college teaching position. I entered my first class filled with enthusiasm and a healthy dose of nerves! I believe that the universe was working from a place of loving intention that fall because in that first class I was met by a beloved group of students, many sophomores, with whom I spent the next three years teaching across different classes and through independent studies and research projects. I often think of the ways we learned and grew alongside one another in that time. When that chapter of my journey came to a close, I realized how symbiotic the professor-student relationship was: we all taught one another because we were all open to learning and growth in community. During those years other students crossed my path who fell into this community as well. I am grateful and extend thanks to every student who showed up in those learning communities through the Hamilton College Education Studies program. I am also so grateful and extend thanks to the many students who were part of my learning communities at Mohawk Valley Community College, Syracuse University, and Utica University. There are students whom I must acknowledge personally, and whom I have had the immense privilege to work closely with across multiple years in Education Studies through things like my teaching, research, and community work. My gratitude is extended to Andres Fluffy Aguilar, Sean Allen, Allison Yoo-Babbitt, Zac Ball, Maddie Beitler, Tyler Bordeau, Julia Booth, Sabrina Boutselis, Estella Brenneman, Jackie Bussgang, Yuri Choi, Ben Cornaglia, Sacharja Cunningham, Pascal Dafanis, Abby Dayton, Gianna Dischiavo, Amari Dumas, Stephanie Fabri, Kathryn Hacker, Grace Heller, Maggie Horne, Diamond Jackson, Olivia Jacobs, Shavell Jones, Donna Le, Emily Liu, Sindy Liu, Fox Maxwell, Rich Marooney, Kelli Mackey, Anna MacDonald, Heidi Mendez, Riley Nichols, Edgar Otero, all of the students from *Education, Teaching, and Social Change*, Shaina Coronel Pazmino, Kate Piacenza, Syon Powell, Joe Pucci, Angélica Ramos, Delta Reyes, Anna Scutt, Missy Segall, Patricia Sheibler, Katherine Spano, Helen Stutsman, Adrian Summers, Aoife Thomas, Anaidys Uribe, Ellie Williams, Hannah Young, and Norman Zupcich. During my time at Hamilton there were several colleagues who fully supported my pedagogical philosophy and inspired me with their own modeling of compassionate ways to work in higher education and across many communities, and I offer my special thanks to Dan Chambliss, Chaise LaDousa, Russell Marcus, Susan Mason, Margo Okazawa-Rey, Chris Willemsen, and Robin Vanderwall.

I have been guided in my own education by faculty, staff, and mentors who were empowering educators for me, and I am so grateful to each of them. Thank you from the bottom of my heart to my New Hartford Central School educators: Carolyn Buckley, Bob Evans, Bob Jones, Michael Klar, Maryann Pomroy Kowalsky, Jerry Pitarresi, Olga Mazzei, and Helen Spector. Thank you to constant supporter, Richard Hunt. Thank you to an early work mentor, Jim Carroll. Thank you to the faculty at Hobart and William Smith Colleges including Jack Harris, Richard Mason, Renee Monson, Dunbar Moody, and former William Smith Dean Betsy Mitchell. Thank you to faculty and staff at Syracuse University including Mary Ann Barker and the whole Cultural Foundations of Education department with special gratitude to Gretchen E. Lopez, Emily Robertson, Dalia Rodriguez, and Ansley T. Erickson. Many thanks also to meaningful faculty mentors Chandra Talpade Mohanty and Marjorie DeVault. Thank you also to the editorial team for education at Peter Lang Publishing, with special gratitude to editor Dani Green for their feedback, support, and guidance.

A tremendous amount of what I wrote in this book stems from my growth as a person and student at Syracuse University. Going back to graduate school in my mid-30s meant there were different conversations happening in academia and new ways of knowing. I experienced the most powerful shifts in my academic life but also my personal life as a result of the loving guidance and intentional mentorship of three women at Syracuse: Gretchen E. Lopez, Chandra Talpade Mohanty, and Marj DeVault. Thank you alone does not capture the impact you have had on my life. It is the greatest privilege to be able to bring your teachings into the communities I am a part of now in higher education classrooms, but also the classrooms of many public communities, as well as the classroom that is my home and my life.

I have been surrounded and lifted tremendously by my peers from the Intergroup Dialogue family at Syracuse. Thank you always to Gretchen E. Lopez for creating the space that we all could grow and transform in, and to Afua Boahene, Wendy Nastasi, Jermaine Soto, Kim Williams Brown, and all of the other members over the years of this radically loving and life-sustaining space that is IGD.

I wrote this book's letter-chapters slowly during the height of the COVID pandemic. This was not a project that I spoke about with many folks until the very end. Each of the friends named here held space for me during the isolating and challenging times of the pandemic. Along the way, they also held space with me for beautiful moments of joy. In sharing themselves with me through friendship they sustained me as a friend, mom, writer, activist, and academic. The space they held for me meant that I was lifted in their love and care in ways that helped me stay the course and keep space to continue this writing project. And so, their love and friendship are a part of this work as well. It is weaved in spirit throughout the writing. I am eternally grateful to each one of them. From the bottom of my heart, I thank Sara Bell, Kim Williams Brown, Erin Breheny Cortese, Jennifer Hurley, Jennifer Matcham, Meredith Moriarty, Dale and Jeannine Ryan, Mary Jo Ryan, Erica Shaw, Colleen Soden, and Mark Soden. I also thank this special group of Clinton and William Smith friends who held intentional spaces through things like Zoom nights, creative birthday celebrations, phone calls, cards, or texts to make sure that during the pandemic we were all holding on: Charity Dreier, Jennifer Goodfriend, Jean Jacobson, Denise Schreppel and Erica Shaw and also Ginny Cogley, Laura Copperwheat, Allison Forbes, and Karen Musante, as well as Amy Schubmehl Barnett, Pam Burkhalter Kalso, Rebecca Scheer, and Jessica Thibeau.

With an outpouring of love, I thank my parents Peter and Linda Madden. Mom and Dad, you have been steady guides in my life who have always modeled love and commitment. Those are two things I strive to bring into my work every day and I am inspired by you both in doing so. My love and gratitude to each of you is immeasurable. Thank you for everything you have done for me and Ronan. I love you. I also lovingly thank Nat Madden, and Peter, Rachel, and Anna Madden. I warmly thank Pat, Alan, and Ariana Mead, my precious grandmother Hazel Willmot and all of my extended Willmot and Madden family members as well as the many, many others who have shown me care over the years. I am so grateful.

But mostly, I thank my son, Ronan Milne. Ronan, you will always be my greatest promise. You inspire me every day to live and love generously, stay the course, and celebrate life in every way. Thank you for always seeing my work and what I write as valuable to the world. Your voice is so strong, and I cannot wait for more people in this world to hear everything that you have to say through the spaces you will create in a way that is most true to you. I love you, Ronan.

· 1 ·

MY SOLIDARITY LETTERS TO YOU: AN INTRODUCTION AND AN INVITATION

Dear Students,

This book is a collection of letters that I have written for you. I name this collection my solidarity letters because I am in solidarity with you and your commitment to having an empowering and transformative journey through higher education. Empowering and transformative may not be the first two words you thought of when thinking of your higher education experience, or perhaps they were the very first things you thought of. Readers will read this book from many different starting points. And that is ok. This book will meet you where you are on your journey. It will give you the language to name some things you have already experienced and some things you have yet to experience. Moreover, it will share messages to inform, inspire, and guide you. This book is not a textbook. There is no single way to navigate higher education. It is written from my own perspective which has been informed by multiple, diverse experiences that have generously informed my ways of knowing. It is a privilege for me to share these ways of knowing with you. I have written each letter with pure intention and heart. I invite you to read them, learn from them, and live informed by them in ways that best serve you and your life.

We may have never met one another, but I know you. "How could she know me?" you ask. For starters, I have shared at least one identity with you: higher education student. I graduated as a sociology major from Hobart and William Smith Colleges (shout out to the class of 1999)! I followed that up with a master's of Public Policy from The George Washington University, then later a master's of Urban Education from Mercy College. Finally, I reached the prize I had kept my eye on for a very long time and graduated with my PhD in Cultural Foundations of Education from Syracuse University where I also earned a certificate of advanced study in Women's and Gender Studies. Let's just say I liked school! And let's also say, school became easier as I understood how to "do school." To society, each of my degrees symbolizes credentials that certify me as "smart." I am stopping right here to say that I know *many* people who do not have a college credential that are extremely smart. I personally think we should value everyone regardless of their credentials. Still, the higher education credential carries a lot of value in the world which is why so many of us are undergraduate or graduate students to begin with. Here is what I want you to know: I have learned that when you peel back the credential you will find layers and layers of complex experiences. My many years of experience studying in higher education, from undergraduate student to graduate student, means that I have some important lessons worth sharing with you.

I am not only in the position to share my knowledge with you, but feel a social responsibility to share my knowledge with you. I'm not talking about book knowledge, but life knowledge. Life knowledge that now has ended up in a book, oh the irony! In addition to being an undergraduate and graduate student, I have worked as a professor since 2010. Currently I teach undergraduate and graduate students. I felt a sense of "I can't believe I am here," when I reached the decade milestone for time spent teaching college students. At that moment, I carved out space to critically reflect on my teaching experiences. I revisited my own jottings on those experiences and stared intently at the notes I had written to myself over the years. Who are these messages for? Why did I write them to myself? What did I not want to forget? What is their purpose? In my heart, I know their purpose is reflected in every letter in the book you hold in your hands (or read on your screen). One purpose of my life's work in education has been to gather up the often silent and invisible methods that are not neatly presented in any syllabus or curriculum, but that once revealed will empower you, keep you thriving, and help you succeed on your terms.

For every day I taught on a college campus, I never stopped learning. From Mohawk Valley Community College, to Syracuse University, to

Excelsior College, and then Hamilton College with my recent tenure track stop at Utica University, I have learned how academic institutions work and how students experience these complex spaces. Trust me, I *know* how hard higher education can be for reasons outside of the actual coursework. From first-hand experiences to my educational equity research, I know that students have multiple, diverse educational experiences prior to college and this positions them to be prepared for college in different ways. For instance, let's take the case of first-generation college students. While the self-identification and definition can vary for complex reasons, a most highly accepted definition of the term first-generation college student is a student whose parent(s) do not hold a four-year college degree. The reality is that many people do not hold a four-year college degree for multiple reasons. Many of those reasons are related to social and economic barriers, while other reasons are related to personal choice and other preferred pathways that don't require a four-year degree. Interestingly, I did not realize there was such a named identity until I was a doctoral student studying education. This is because the term was not largely established in higher education until the late 1990s which is the time I graduated from college. In retrospect, I see now how understanding that identity while in college would have helped me and others better understand and navigate higher education experiences as a first-generation college student. I have many college memories where I had that slight hunch that my peers knew something that I did not know. I couldn't grasp it. I didn't have the language for it. From the confident ways some folks interacted with faculty, to the finely-tuned approaches to class preparation and engagement, to even knowing the timeline for how the process and pathway should unfold. For example, I recall senior spring listening to people in the college cafe talk about where they were heading for work after graduation. I sat stunned thinking "How do they already know what they are doing next year?" I slowly learned that my assumption that you had to wait to start the job search until *after* graduation when you had your diploma in hand was uniformed. While I do not regret the open road approach I found myself on, or how long it took me to navigate those windy roads, in retrospect having an overview of the land ahead of time could have positioned me to make guided decisions about my options and relieved some stress of the unknown. This may have also made me feel slightly more in control of my journey.

Identities such as first-generation college student and other marginalized identities often position students to be less versed in the language of best practices for how to "do school." This is not a negative reflection of the student themselves because people don't know what they don't know. When you don't have access to certain ways of knowing such as practices for "doing school" in higher education then there is a systemic barrier in place that can negatively impact your knowing and by extension your doing. In the field of sociology, terms for this know-how include social and cultural capital. Even some students without marginalized identities may lack this language if they are impacted by people who undermine their self-determination for college or, quite the opposite, by people who very much value their self-determination for college but still have their own college knowledge gaps. Let's be clear, this means that students who lack access to the unwritten practices of "doing school" are missing information that will benefit them. Everyone deserves that information. I want you to have it! As a public scholar, my work is fully intended for *you*. By writing these letters to you, it is my intention to share the many unwritten practices of "doing school," work to level the higher education playing field so you can claim your education, and support your thriving as a successful student on *your* terms. It is true that people do not know what they do not know. Or they may know some things but in ways that are incomplete. At the end of each letter written to you in this book is a list of "know-how" strategies I have curated for you based on things I have come to know to lift, help, and support many students. They are meant as a guide and of course are not exclusive or exhaustive. It is my hope that they can help you move forward in actionable ways that support you and let you thrive in your life.

This book, these solidarity letters, is written for you. I can tell you these messages have helped the students I have worked with at every college and university. In my classes, I share knowledge about how to "do school." I name things that some may already know, but many do not. I have heard from countless students across the years who remember the messages and experienced positive outcomes as a result of them. I want these messages to not be bound by the walls of one classroom and one institution. As an educational equity scholar, I know that the road toward equity and education is long. The messages in this book are intentional attempts by myself as a person in a community of folks committed to helping pave that road so the students coming up the road can have a smoother, safer, just, and more rewarding journey.

The title of this book claims these letters will empower and transform your higher education journey. I believe they can and I hope they will. I hope you read the letters that follow and feel seen and supported by them. Some of the letters are intended to support you by assisting you with navigating how to "do school." Some of the letters are meant to support you by emotionally lifting you when times are hard, which they may be. All of the letters are meant to help you survive, thrive, and succeed during your years in higher education and in your life at large. I stand with you on your journey. I share and support your commitment to your education. This book is solidarity in action and these are my solidarity letters to you.

Warmly,
Professor Madden

· 2 ·

GET NOTICED AND COME CENTER

Dear Students,

When I was in my first year of graduate school at Syracuse University, I attended a new student orientation for members of my doctoral program. I remember how nervous I felt sitting in the rectangular room filled with aspiring PhDs. I also recall my curiosity about the surrounding faculty who sat confidently before us and embodied the very thing I dreamed of being, a professor. I listened to all of the remarks and suggestions from the faculty about how to orient ourselves to the program. I stockpiled the list of expectations and responsibilities in my mind as I mentally prepared to work my hardest on this journey. I cannot recall all that was shared that day. However, there was one remark that has stayed with me ever since that humid August afternoon in the third floor conference room of Huntington Hall. Sitting on a craftsman style sofa was a new faculty member, a historian of education, Dr. Ansley Erickson. Dr. Erickson shared advice with us that had been shared with her and in the spirit of paying it forward, I am here to share that message with you. It is the first message in this book because it has been one of the most important ones I have received across my education: *Get noticed.*

When Dr. Erickson said "Get noticed" to that room of students, I remember feeling like a gust of wind had whipped across my face. *What did she just say?* I thought. *Get noticed?* My first reaction was one of surprise. All I could think was, *How bold.* Then the following thoughts flooded my mind: *Who am I to get noticed? Why would I go and do a thing like that? Wouldn't that be so self-serving? So egotistical and showy? So unhumble?* I had never been the type of person to intentionally try to *get* noticed. That said, I desperately wanted to *be* noticed. I was the young student in school that worked so hard at everything I did and hoped upon hopes that my teachers would notice me. But to plant my feet front and center and name my gifts and talents, communicate my needs, and ask for what I wanted? No. Not me. I unknowingly connected being noticed to being good and so being noticed was where I put all of my feelings of affirmation and validation. I had not yet realized that the first person I needed to have notice me, affirm me, and validate me and my work was my very own self. As a result, I internalized many feelings of low self-worth that often grew into self-doubt when I felt unnoticed by people such as my teachers, coaches, instructors, or professors. When my grade school teacher went up and down the line of students at dismissal with her smiley face stamp and pressed the blue ink down on the small hands of everyone who wrote their name perfectly that day, I held out my hand and waited. My insides would crumble as she passed by me. I wanted so badly for her to notice me and to see how hard I had worked to write each of the eight letters of my name. On the day I finally received the blue smiley face on my hand I felt a rush of happiness. I felt worthy. How important it would have been for me to know then that while my crooked letters may have been unworthy of the teacher's stamp of approval, that did not mean that I was unworthy as a person. Yet these are the messages that students internalize. Our early educational experiences shape us and impact how we experience our education going forward. For me, being noticed brought me to the center, and not being noticed made me feel pushed to the outside margins. The margins are that outermost space in a classroom. You can't see them, but they are there. The problem is that once you are on the margins, you become the observer to everyone else's experiences and over time it seems like the stone is cast. To move toward the center can feel impossible. The people at the center seem to stay at the center. They become noticed and secure their place as people who are valued. While the people on the margins seem to stay on the margins, wondering when their turn will come to be noticed, included, and valued. So there I was in graduate school walking the tightrope where on one side was the student waiting for affirmation from others to deem myself worthy or valuable of other's esteem, and on the other side was the student who had Dr. Erickson's words echoing in her ears: *Get noticed.* Where would I land in graduate school? Would I be a doer or a watcher? And who was going to make that call? The bottom line was having to ask myself, was I going to wait for others to decide if and when I was worthy of being noticed? Or was I going to tell myself "You and your work are worthy of being noticed," and make a commitment to *get noticed.* Who was I authentically doing my work for?

I decided I would not be complicit in my own marginalization. Now, truth be told there are many people who are not complicit in their own marginalization and are *still* marginalized in the classroom. That's not a reason to get complicit, but it is a reason to be aware and understand how that happens and what to do when it happens. Getting noticed requires that you first start seeing yourself on *your* terms. How can we expect to be noticed by others if we are unwilling to first do the work of listening to and taking notice of our own unique selves? No one knows you better than yourself. It is up to each of us to tell the world who we are, what we do, what we need, what we want, and what we can contribute. So learn it, know it, own it, and share it. All of this said, no space is perfect, and this includes education. Sad but true, you or others may encounter people that do not value you or your identity enough to create spaces where you can move from the margins to the center. This is unjust and unacceptable. Yet the reality is that so many people exist in unjust spaces that do not support them. I encourage you to seek counsel from someone on campus, be it a trusted mentor, adviser, professor, staff, or administrator, on how to address what you are facing so you can thrive in all educational spaces. If that applies to you and you find yourself in one such space, then just remember that you do not belong on the margins. You belong in the center. Claim your space in the center.

Over time I learned that getting noticed and coming center requires specific things in higher education. Ask yourself questions like the ones I learned to ask myself:

(1) Am I challenging myself to speak in class? If not, am I willing to make a plan to increase my participation?

(2) When I go to class and meetings with my professors, do I show up fully prepared? For instance, do I show up to class with key points and questions that I can raise for discussion? Also, do I bring an agenda of items to my office hours visits and lead the meeting based on the needs of myself and my work? Remember, whoever calls the meeting should lead the meeting.

(3) Do I give myself time to reflect on today but also dream of tomorrow? Do I sit with my feelings and thoughts, and my fears and hopes, so that I have a sense of what path I want to keep on even if it's not perfectly clear to me yet?

(4) As I develop a sense of what my path looks like and the direction I want to head, do I intentionally identify the faculty and staff at my school whose commitments and work align with my own interests? Do I purposefully communicate my interests and availability so that when opportunities are created that require things like research assistance, which they will, then I am a person who comes to mind? Or, so that when I have an opportunity that I want to create on campus like organizing an event, then I know who might support my efforts?

It is crucial to do the work of getting noticed and working to move to the center in one's own education. If it's not being done then one must ask, "Why am I not doing it? Are there things I don't know about the process that I need to know? Will I commit to learning those things and trying them?" Over time, I learned that my own interests, ideas, and work have never belonged on the margins. Trust me when I tell you this: neither do yours. Though remember again that there may not always be people creating spaces for you to move center. So, with that knowledge I encourage you, in your own life, to boldly let it begin with you. The chapters ahead will help you understand best practices for getting noticed and coming to the center in higher education. You are not alone in doing this important work.

Dear students, please hear me on this. I wish I had the tools to let it begin with me earlier in my higher education experience. Let it begin with you now from wherever you stand. You cannot afford to go unnoticed in this world. And the world cannot afford for you to go unnoticed either. Do you remember the very first thing I thought to myself after Dr. Erickson told me and my peers to get noticed? I thought, *How bold*. And I was right. It is bold to get noticed. It is one of the boldest, most radical things you can do. And guess what? It is also essential to get noticed. It is necessary. You are worthy of getting noticed. The act of getting noticed is self-serving in the most important way. If you do not serve yourself then who else will?

To every student, I say focus on getting noticed, coming center and claiming your space in the center. Come center on campus, in the classroom, at work, with your research, on the field, rink, court or water, at the conference, in your clubs and organizations, in the paper or journal, and in your community. Through the boldness of your being, I urge you to *get* noticed so you can *be* noticed. You are worthy. You are deserving. The world eagerly awaits for the promise that is you.

In solidarity,
Professor Madden

Getting Noticed "Know-How" Strategies for "Doing School"

(1) Tell yourself that you deserve to get noticed. Repeat it again and again.

(2) Write down a list of how you see yourself and how you think the world sees you. Take inventory. Do these ways of seeing align? Would you like to be seen in different ways? Name those ways and visualize yourself getting noticed in those ways. For example, "I see myself as someone with lots to say. The world sees me as quiet." From here you can see these two ways of seeing oneself do not align. While this student should not care about others' opinions of them, they can still care about people not making assumptions about what they can or cannot do based on seeing them as quiet. So, the student could name for themselves that they want to be seen as someone who while quiet still has important contributions to make and visualize demonstrating that to others. The student might say, "If I struggle with class participation then I will email my professor after class and tell them my thoughts on that day's lecture so I get noticed as someone who has important things to say and is willing to say them." Or, "If I struggle with class participation then I will show up to class having read the assigned reading and written down three main points from the reading, one critical passage, and one question that can guide my class engagement in real time."

(3) Write down a list of things that you value most about yourself. Next, write down the things you are doing to demonstrate the value of those things to others. For example, "I value my interest in learning and researching the experiences of parenting students. I have communicated this value to my professor who is an expert in the field and asked her for resources. I will ask her if she will consider being my Independent Study advisor next semester because I want to immerse myself in this topic."

(4) If you are not doing anything to demonstrate what you value then once you've written down the things you value you should write down your plans to demonstrate that value to others in the future. For example, "I value learning about Oceanography. I am not doing well on the class tests so I need to go to office hours to let my professor know that I value the content but I am struggling on exams and need extra help."

(5) Make a list of the people you interact with regularly in college/university from professors to coaches to peers. Commit to proactively developing intentional communication with these folks knowing that it will be different for each person. Keep it simple. Be clear and direct. Reflect, regroup, and remain. Even when it's uncomfortable you should keep communication growing and you will find the ways you are noticed will grow too. Remember people aren't mind readers. Get noticed by giving people the glasses with the lens that you want them to see you through instead of letting them view you through their glasses and a lens that might not see you clearly.

(6) Are you centered in your educational experiences? Does your voice come center in the classroom? How about your leadership in co-curricular spaces? If you are being taught, coached, or advised by someone who actively creates spaces where no matter what you do you still experience barriers to moving center and claiming your educational experience then talk to someone you trust and get advice on navigating the problematic situation.

(7) Closing as we began: you deserve to get noticed. You do not have to wait for others to notice you. Close by naming yourself as the writer in control of your life and this chapter that is higher education. Your commitment to getting noticed means that you write the words. Pen in hand. Hand to paper. Reveal yourself. Get noticed.

(8) Trust yourself.

· 3 ·

BUILD YOUR CIRCLE OF SUPPORT

Dear Students,

I grew a great deal in my first five years of college teaching. That growth was due to the generously open students I encountered in the classroom. It was in that space that I developed the practice of sharing the knowledge and experiences I had gained through the years, so that my students could collect whatever support strategies might be useful to them along their higher education journey. One lesson that I have learned as a professor is that so many students are learning without support. There are many reasons for this. Some folks are used to having to do things on their own or are socialized to think that there is greater value to being independent rather than interdependent. Whatever the reason, many students lack understanding of the power of community and also lack skills for building networks. Years after my first teaching job, when I cross paths with my former students, there is one message of mine they most often say has stayed with them and brought positive change to their life: *Build your circle of support.*

I never felt more supported in my education than when I was a PhD student at Syracuse University. Yet I know that I attended many academic institutions that had a wealth of resources: a nationally ranked public school, a liberal arts college, and two reputable graduate programs at the masters level.

Let me be very clear, I did experience moments of support in each of those spaces, and I remain grateful to those people. Yet my time at Syracuse was different. Why? The difference for me was that I was in my thirties and had a better grasp on what supports I needed. There is a beautiful saying with obscure origins but most often attributed to Buddha that goes, "When the student is ready, the teacher appears." I was *ready* to intentionally gather my supports one by one and build them around me. As a result, the teachers began to appear. The only thing that is bittersweet for me in writing those words is that I am certain I must have been surrounded by so many *teachers* in my life whose impression I will never know. I think that readiness comes with time and maturity, so in that way I can go easy on myself. But I also think that readiness comes with knowledge that gets transferred to some of us earlier if we happen to cross paths with someone who knows it and is willing to share it. So, I wish to share this knowledge with you now so that you can be *ready* and that the teachers of your life: professors, friends, peers, family, coaches, leaders, community members, and so forth, may *appear* for you to learn from, gain strength from, and celebrate with for the important work that is the life you continue to grow.

To build your circle of support means that you have to think critically about what you need. When I share this message with my students I begin by drawing a person on the board. I ask them, as I'll ask you, to do the same on a separate piece of paper. Begin with yourself at the center then write the names of the people who are in your life and are a part of your circle of support in a circle around you. For some students, names of family members fill up the page. For others it is a partner, boyfriend, girlfriend, or other close friends. Over the years I have seen the names of many mentors, coaches, and spiritual leaders, and of course, teachers. The second part of the exercise often goes something like this: name the support that the person gives you. The one thing in common across the many names that have shown up on all of those pieces of paper is that those were people in the students' lives who had shown them *care*. Those were the people who students felt "had their back" or took time to know them as individuals on the good days as well as the bad days. Those were the people who recognized that the students needed support. Those were the people in the circle.

Dear students, spend time identifying who is currently in your circle of support. Think of the reasons behind why they are there. Acknowledge them for the support they give. Then, spend time thinking about what support you need as a student to help you figure out if you need to widen your circle and include others. I would imagine you will find that others will be needed. It would be impossible for a handful of people to meet all of our needs, especially when we are growing and our needs are changing. What support will you need to keep you on *your* path? This exercise often raises awareness. Some students are not sure what support they need to keep them on their path let alone get them to the destination. If this is you, you are not alone. Most students know they are working toward a degree, but are still in the process of figuring out their undergraduate majors or graduate concentration areas, let alone career fields. If that sounds familiar, accept that you are where you are at the moment, but set quiet time aside to think about your vision for a life that will sustain you. If you are in this place, then you may need a person to support you as a mentor. This would be a person who is patient, a good listener, and perspective taker. This is a person that understands how much is learned through the *process* of doing, and who commits to helping you find your way with respect to *your* experience. This person should not be helping you by convincing you to do things *their* way. You are not living their life. They are not living yours. Their way may *inform* your way, but this person should be the type to know that you are the driver and they are a passenger on your journey. If you know this is what you need, spend time reflecting on all of the many people in your life. Which ones might fill this role well? Once you have some people in mind, you might ask them to meet with you so you can explain where you are on your path, and communicate that you are looking for people to support you as you stay on your path and work toward your goals. Tell them how you see them as someone who might be able to support you based on what you need and also on the characteristics they have that make them a good fit. Then, ask them if they are interested and willing to be this person for you. In most cases, people will say yes! In other cases, it might be that people are *interested* but unwilling due to circumstances that have nothing to do with you, such as not having enough time.

Sometimes the people who care for us the *most* are the people who want to be the driver of our journey. I am a mom and I get this completely! There is something so comfortable about thinking that I could buckle my teenage son up next to me on life's highway and deliver him safely to adulthood to an amazing destination where his dreams could be realized. But I know this would also mean he would arrive at *my* version of the "amazing destination" without his own experiences to help him learn how to thrive once he arrives there. If you find yourself in the passenger seat of your own life, I encourage you to have a heart to heart talk with the "driver," if you feel that would be best for you. Identify how much you know they care about you, and how much that care has supported you. Tell them you still need them to care for you, but communicate to them if you want to, or need to, take the wheel. Remind them that if you take the wheel that doesn't mean you are kicking them out of the car and to the curb! Be aware that is what this conversation might feel like to them, so it is on you to communicate that this doesn't mean that you don't need them or haven't appreciated them. This might be a difficult conversation. People's feelings may be hurt. We end up in higher education because in addition to our hard work, other people have likely invested decades of time, energy, and resources into us. The driver might be financing your education and feel a sense of ownership. It is important for people to know that you are not rejecting them as people, but rather you are recognizing how important they are and you are holding them in your life as someone with whom you want to ride *alongside*. If anything, they become some of the most important people on your journey. These people are often the ones that can anchor you to some of the earlier versions of your best self. They can remind you of who you are, of where you came from, of your dreams, and your values. The goal is not to remove these people from your circle of support, unless of course they are toxic to your growth and undermine or invalidate your lived experience, but you must be the one to decide that. Instead, keep space for those that care about you, but make space for others who can also meet your developing needs and support your growth.

I encourage you to do a few things. Now that you have thought about the support you need, it is up to *you* to build your circle of support. Perhaps you are interested in transferring from a large university to a small private college, or from a community college to a four-year institution, or between graduate programs. Maybe you are curious about working in many different fields but have no idea what steps you would even need to take to get on that path! Say you have a research project in mind but have no idea how to begin the study. Or you might be in student loan debt finding yourself unsure of how you will pay back your existing loans, let alone take out new ones if needed. In your current circle there may not be people who have the knowledge and resources to guide you, but *you* can do your homework and start researching who might. Start first by telling things to the universe: talk to trusted advisers, professors, mentors, friends, and peers. Share with people what you are thinking about, wondering about, and questioning. Perhaps you want to know the best path to become an engineer, or how to gain financial literacy so you can make a plan for paying off student loan debt, or best practices for community-based projects. Ask folks if they know anyone who might have some information on these things. Gather names from contacts, and use the internet to search local people in your area beginning by starting where you are at your own institution. From there: contact them!

I urged my students to come up with a list like this with names and contact information and send three emails a week asking people for an informal meeting by phone or in-person to create their circles of support with intention. I urge you to do the same! You won't hear back from all, and of the ones you do hear back from not all will be able to support you. Even if they can't support you now, it's good to know that people have long memories. Years later you may find yourself applying for a position and someone there may recall that you reached out a few years prior. This will communicate your intention, dedication, and careful preparation to enter the field. Think of it like fishing, the more times you cast your line the more likely you are to get a bite! In your email, I suggest introducing yourself and your interests and goals, sharing what you know about the person (including if the person was recommended to you by someone else), and then sharing what you would like to know from them. You may be surprised to discover how many people really want to share what they know and are committed to helping the people coming up the road behind them. By the end of the semester the vast majority of my students had established new contacts and new networks. More often than not, my students had built their circle of support. The wonderful thing about circles of support is that they can be ever changing, and there is no magic number of people required to be in them. I believe that you can do this building, and that it will greatly benefit you.

There is a candle holder called "The Circle of Friends" that I see from time to time in gift shops. It has always caught my eye. Formed from pottery is a circle of people with arms locked facing the candle. Imagine yourself as the flame. You are the light. Build your circle of support around you and you may be guarded and protected by others. They will watch as your flame goes out from time to time, yet they will still face you in the darkness. As much of a gift that each of these people will be to you along your journey, you will also be a gift to them. They will watch as your flame flickers and burns bright, and they will bask in the glow of your light. Through it all, you will know that you are never, ever alone. Build your circle of support. May your flame shine long and bright.

In solidarity,
Professor Madden

Building Your Circle of Support "Know-How" Strategies For "Doing School"

(1) Get a piece of paper and put your name in the center. Draw a circle around your name. Write the names of the people who actively support you and your higher education journey around the line of the circle.

(2) Think of who else you would like to add to your circle that is not listed. These could be professors that you feel a connection with, adults that work in the field you would eventually like to work in, or other people that participate in things you are committed to and work to thrive at in your life. These might also include people you have never met. For example, if your roommate's mother works in publishing and that is your dream industry then add her name and ask your roommate if you could reach out to their mom about publishing. Or, say you have always wanted to live in New York City and work in the Arts at Lincoln Center. Research the many different opportunities at Lincoln Center even if you are years away from being on the job market. Find out who is doing the work you want to do there and send an introduction email to introduce yourself, express your long-term goal, and ask if you could be in touch with them to set up an informational meeting to learn more about this potential career path. Planting these seeds of interest and curiosity are important!

(3) Create a timeline and challenge yourself to build your circle by reaching out to at least one person in your circle every other week to build a connection. You could do this through email, text, or an invitation to meet and talk virtually or in-person. Be intentional and communicate to them that they are a person who you would like to learn from and gain guidance from. Don't hesitate to tell them if there is something specific you are looking for help with.

(4) Create opportunities to learn from the people in your circle. For example, a student in the field of finance might invite a person they know in the field for a coffee and ask questions about what advice they have for them and lessons they have learned along their own journey. Try to connect with one person per month for a meet up. Keep notes and reach back out with a thank you and follow up to keep the relationship moving forward.

(5) Every few months reflect on who the people are that take space in your circle. Is there anyone missing? Circles of support will grow with you in your higher education journey because you will be growing and your needs for support will change and grow too. Keep reflecting and revisiting. Above all, keep communicating with authenticity, integrity, and care.

(6) Tell the universe! Resolve to always reflect on your needs and communicate them to yourself and to others. If people specifically know what you need or hope for then they are more likely to show up to support you.

(7) Practice gratitude. Know that circles of support are places of space held by people managing their own lives. If you are the flame in the middle and you only take all of the oxygen from the people in the circle then eventually your flame will extinguish. Gratitude is extremely important. Show it. Give back through sincere communications of affirmation of the relationship and its impact.

(8) Reflect on the ways people hold or held space for you in your circle and commit to being a person in someone else's circle of support when you are asked and able to do so. But don't always wait for the direct ask. Look around you, there are people who would appreciate you showing up for them and may not have the tools to reach out and ask. We are all in this together.

(9) Trust yourself.

· 4 ·

THE SIGNIFICANCE OF FACULTY RELATIONSHIPS: FROM OFFICE HOURS TO RECOMMENDATIONS

Dear Students,

The spring of my senior year in college, I sat in my sociology class and listened to Professor Jack Harris share something that brought me to full attention. According to Professor Harris, we should all have at least three faculty members who could speak very well about us in letters of recommendation for future jobs or graduate school. When I tell you I woke up quick after I heard that message, I mean *quick*. I sat there trying to think of three faculty members who would be able to write me my letters. As a senior, this was a precarious moment for someone without much time left to get to know faculty! Which of my professors really *knew* me? I wondered. At that moment, I could come up with two people. Sure, I had been part of small classes, and had taken courses with the same professor on multiple occasions, but beyond my modest class participation and writing samples, what else had I demonstrated about myself to my professors? Not too much. That being said, until Professor Harris shared that message with our class, I was not aware that intentionally building relationships with professors was something that I needed to do. At that point, I wasn't even aware of how future applications would work, let alone fully grasp the preparation needed before being at a place to ask someone to be a reference. You may read that and think, how naive! Or you may relate to that and be embarrassed to admit it, especially when you realize other people somehow already know those things. Don't be. Remember, you don't know what you don't know until someone flat out tells you. Professor Harris was the first person to ever tell me that, and I remain grateful to him for that knowledge to this day. I don't take that exchange for granted. I feel a responsibility to keep sharing in large part because of the impact that one moment had on me. As a professor I spend a lot of time thinking about what I am doing to prepare my students for the post-college and post-grad school world. There is no way about it, you can get a 4.0 grade point average but if you do not have strong recommendations about you as a *whole* person then you will be at a disadvantage. Now don't panic if like me you find yourself learning this a little later on … there is always time. As much as I'm thinking about the ways I am preparing my students for life post-college, I urge them to think about the ways *they* are preparing themselves for life post-college. One crucial part of that preparatory work is: *Get to know your professors and get them to know you.*

I was not the type of college student to intentionally get to know my professors. It wasn't that I didn't want to know them. I just didn't know how to get to know them nor was I especially certain that as a student I was supposed to be taking up more of their time. There were always a few students who seemed to know certain professors really well and on a first name basis. I wondered how that type of relationship even came about. Now as a professor I have my hunches: through office hours. Office hours are the designated hours each week that professors hold to meet with students in their office and support their academic and personal growth by discussing the course material, answering questions, and offering strategies to support everything from test prep to paper revisions as well as a listening ear during moments of challenge and supporting students as whole people. Traditionally, office hours have been held in a professor's physical office space on campus. Today you will find there is more flexibility around where office-hour meetings take place. Many professors still use their physical office for these meetings and provide you with the office location in the syllabus. Some professors hold office hours through virtual video meetings and provide you with the link to their virtual office location in the syllabus. Others consider email communications or phone calls to count as an office-hour meeting as well. Some professors have established time frames for these meetings. This means that you will need to know the days and times and the policy for how to meet with them. While they are called office "hours" you will rarely have an hour of time. Many professors have students scheduled in 15, 20, or 30 minute blocks to hold a space and reduce wait times. Other professors have open office hours at a scheduled time where students can "drop-in" unannounced and take the time they need. If that's the case with your professors then bring things to work on as there can often be a line and an extended wait. Some professors, especially in the Science and Math fields, also hold small-group office hours when working on labs or problem sets. Some students find this very helpful. Others find it challenging. If you find it challenging then request a 1:1 meeting. Others may only have "by appointment" office hours which relies on you to request a meeting for a mutually agreeable date and time. Some may have a combination of both. You may also have a Teaching Assistant (TA) for your class and be assigned to office-hour meetings with them as well. This is a regular practice. Often these are graduate students or undergraduates who have demonstrated mastery of the content. You should find information about office hours at the very top of the syllabus. Your professor should also communicate to you how to sign-up to meet, which could be asking them in-person at the beginning or end of class, by email, or through an online scheduling platform (many professors will add a scheduling link to their email signature or in the syllabus). If you don't see this information listed and it isn't discussed in early class meetings then you should make it a priority to ask the professor about where and when their office hours will be held and how you should schedule them.

As an undergraduate, I thought of office hours only as what you attended if you needed clarification on something and now I know that they are a space that offers so much more. Begin with thinking of office hours as a space to make meaningful connections and build a relationship with your professor. Some of my professors had mandatory office hours and required each of us to go for 15 minutes at the beginning of the semester to introduce ourselves. Brilliant idea. Beyond the introduction, this helped me and others get over the intimidating barrier of getting to their office to begin with which for some students can be the hardest part! After all, showing up is often half the battle. There are many reasons students don't show up. Stress and anxiety are a huge reason. For me, even those introductory meetings were stressful and anxiety-ridden and I know many students manage such moments of anxiety as well. From figuring out where the office is, navigating new buildings, the uncomfortable moment when the professor's door is closed and you are plagued with worry about whether to knock or not to knock? I once sat for 30 minutes outside of a professor's door because I could hear her talking on the phone and didn't know what to do. Even though we had a scheduled meeting. Turns out she was talking on the phone while waiting for me to show up!

She felt terrible when she opened the door and found me waiting there. She asked me how long I had been waiting and I told her. She said she wished I had knocked. As a professor, I notice that when my door is closed for reasons including trying to eat a quick lunch, and I see the shadow of a body outside the frosted window next to the door just standing there, I have also thought, *why don't they knock?* But then I remember, we don't always know what we are supposed to do in these moments. It is uncertain. Sometimes when I have opened my office door I catch a slight nervous breath taken in by the students as if they are trying to figure out what to do. Other times I have found students walking away because they decided not to knock and I call out for them to please come back!

What I have learned from my time as a student and as a professor is that going to office hours is extremely difficult for many students. It is intimidating, uncomfortable, and sometimes awkward because there are no rules for how to do these meetings well. But, what I have also learned is that if you visit a few times, it does get easier. Teaching at a small college afforded me many office-hour meetings with the same students over many years. I have observed students who felt uncomfortable for the first handful of visits now have such confidence when they visit me in my office. Repeated visits from students have been an opportunity for them to know more about my thoughts on everything from the assigned reading to the cafe lunch! It is here that we get to know one another beyond our titles of professor and student, and come to understand each other better as people. More importantly, by students doing the work of visiting my office they have created wonderful opportunities for me to learn more about them in ways that I am not always able to in the classroom over a semester, and especially not in larger classes. I learn about their summer plans, and hopes for internships and jobs. I learn about their on-campus commitments, their club meetings, concerts, competitions, and games, and it is then that I am most often invited to come watch them and cheer them on: which I do. Nothing is more enjoyable to me than seeing a student thriving in other areas of their life outside of the classroom, especially because I know how inter-connected curricular and co-curricular experiences can be. I am also constantly reminded by them how much it means to have my support when I attend. To think, it all began in office hours.

For other students, students who may be less vocal in class, office hours are cherished meetings where I can hear how they are engaging the course material, and understand and work with them on their challenges. The number one challenge students identify during office hours is their fear of speaking in class. This is true across every institution I have taught at. Office hours have been an opportunity to set up strategies to address the fear of speaking, such as pre-planning a moment when a student will be asked to participate in the form of a "cold-call" in front of the whole class even though the student knows the moment that I will be calling on them ahead of time. The rest of the class is none the wiser, while the student builds their confidence in speaking. When you do this often enough, eventually students start volunteering to talk on their own. If your professor doesn't offer that as a strategy for you, then consider asking them if they might. All of the visits from students to my office hours have built a connection that has been more sustainable in the classroom and through the years by email updates and campus visits. And so, when the time comes for students to request a letter of recommendation, I am able to do so from a place of deep meaning and understanding, and my letters reflect that.

Dear students, I know office hours can be an uncomfortable, unstructured moment where you may not be sure what to expect or what you are supposed to talk about. If you feel that way, try telling your professor. They are not mind readers and will appreciate your honesty. They will likely work to make your visit a more comfortable one. In the "know-how" strategies section at the end of this letter you will find guiding points for making your visit one that will help you thrive as a student and build a positive relationship with your professor. Following these guiding points will very likely increase the meaningfulness of your relationships with your professors and this will most likely result in a more meaningful higher education experience for you. This will also mean that when it comes time to ask for letters of recommendation that you will have many people who can write about you as a *whole* person. And it bears repeating once more, don't forget to express gratitude. When it comes to writing letters of recommendation, thank you notes (electronic is fine!) still matter, and professors do remember. Writing letters of recommendation is extremely time-consuming, and most professors take this investment of time and energy quite seriously. Remember to not only thank folks, but to let them know how things turned out because we are rooting for you! If it did not turn out in your favor, tell us that too. Everyone has been rejected at some point or another. Chin up. Communicating that news may lead you to find someone willing to mentor you through the difficult moment and help prepare you for new opportunities ahead. Finally, because there are many people who feel this way, and in case you are one of them, please memorize this line: You are not a burden. I am aware that many students feel they are burdening professors by asking for their time. So, in case you didn't know, office-hour meetings and writing letters of recommendation for students they ethically can recommend are part of a professor's job responsibilities. You are not a burden if you need to ask to meet with a professor outside of their scheduled office hours. If your professor's only office hours conflict with your work shift, then communicate that to them and see if accommodations can be made. In some cases, there may be no solutions to that dilemma, so setting up electronic communication for your questions and thought sharing will be imperative.

Ask yourself which professors you want to build a relationship with during your higher education journey. Who will be your three letter writers? Professors will write what you have shown them about yourself. Do you want a strong referee? That means you must work on being a strong student. This does not mean you have to be perfect. But you should demonstrate some sort of growth be it academic or personal. And where would that growth be demonstrated to them, you ask? I think by now you know the answer. Go to office hours. Get to know your professors. Let them get to know you.

In solidarity,
Professor Madden

Building Relationships with Faculty "Know-How" Strategies for "Doing School"

Office-Hour Visits

(1) Go to office hours. Schedule in your calendar brief introductory office-hour visits to each professor during the first two weeks of the semester. Then follow through and take the first step by showing up. You'll be relieved once you have established where the office is and realized that outside of the classroom your professors are people too. Getting in this introductory visit early will make future visits less stressful when you really need them. It may feel uncomfortable but your comfort zone will stretch with each visit. You can do it!

(2) Have an agenda for your office-hour meeting. This gives you structure and shows that you are prepared and organized. This does not have to be something super formal, but you want to know what you are aiming to accomplish. Knowing what you want to discuss is important, so communicate it first and go from there. You can even communicate

the purpose of your visit (e.g., reviewing feedback on a paper) when you ask for a meeting so that your professor can best prepare for your visit. If you asked for an office-hour meeting then consider yourself in the driver seat and lead the meeting, or at least be prepared to do so with your agenda in mind.

(3) Plan to visit office hours when preparing to write a paper. Share your paper thesis and/or outline for feedback *before* you start writing. If your professor will not give you feedback on your thesis then you should visit your school's writing center. A strong paper relies on a strong thesis statement. You want to be certain you have written a thesis that will be easily identifiable and able to be developed. An outline is a paper's roadmap. Sharing this with your professor can create an opportunity to think about what road you are going to take your reader on and if you need to make any adjustments. If your professor can't or won't give you feedback, then there again, go to the writing center.

(4) Use your office-hour meeting to build meaningful connections by discussing things you learned in class that are significant to you. Where there are gaps in your knowledge identified on exams or assignments, ask for clarification and demonstrate your commitment to understand the content for the sake of learning the content and not only for the sake of the grade. Talk about things that are unclear to you and build on the things that are clear. Make connections between what you are learning and your own lived experiences.

(5) In office hours, relationship-building can extend beyond the course content. Take time to share what you are involved in on campus and extend an invitation to them to attend your events and support you as a whole student. Many professors will genuinely appreciate this invitation. Name things you hope to do during and after college, and especially name anything that involves working with them on their research. On that note, ask them what projects they are working on and if you are interested in doing that specific work, tell them! Remember, professors aren't mind readers and you need to get noticed. So, communicate and name what's important to you and where you see links between what is important to you and what is important to them. They will appreciate this communication! It can also be the very information sharing that leads to future opportunities for you!

(6) Show gratitude for your professor's time and feedback. You might be surprised at the number of students who do not respond to hellos and goodbyes let alone say thank you for the information offered during the meeting. Yes, you are entitled to your professor's time in office hours, but gratitude reflects a lot about you and will be noticed and appreciated.

References and Letters of Recommendation

(1) Make a list of professors who you are confident would write you a *strong* letter of recommendation. If there are not three people on that list then think of which faculty members you have felt a connection with and make a commitment to yourself to work on building a relationship with them where they can get to know you as a whole student beyond just a grade. Cast a wide net so that you can ask different people for different letters since some people won't be available or won't be the best fit for every one of your future applications.

(2) Ask for your letter of recommendation as early as possible. Most professors require two weeks minimum notice with many requiring a month. You can and should still ask for a letter even if your deadline is sooner than that but just be prepared that some may not be able to write on such short notice. If you don't have the specifics yet you can still communicate that you are considering applying for something and communicate what it is and the approximate timeline. Be sure to ask if they can write you a "strong letter of recommendation" or be a "strong reference." If they can't, they should tell you and then you can ask someone else.

(3) Once someone agrees to write you a letter you should give them supporting materials to help them write the strongest letter for you. Provide them with your current resume. Also give them a brief summary that tells them why you are applying for the position or program; how you are uniquely prepared to meet the needs or requirements of the position or program through examples of your talents and strengths; and how the position or program will position you to meet your long-term goals.

(4) Send to those writing letters of recommendation a warm reminder a week in advance as well as a two-day in advance reminder. Reminders

are appreciated by busy professors who may have lost track of the
deadline.

(5) Communicate gratitude to your recommenders promptly (within 48
hours) and let them know the outcome!

(6) Trust yourself.

· 5 ·

YOUR VOICE MATTERS: ADDRESSING FEARS OF SPEAKING IN CLASS, DISRUPTING YOUR SILENCE, AND ENGAGING YOUR VOICE

Dear Students,

I rarely spoke in my college classes. The tides shifted for me in graduate school, but I know that even graduate students struggle with speaking in class. In college, if I did speak it was most often because a professor randomly called on me, so I had to come up with something to say. In those moments, my voice was anchored to feelings of embarrassment that my thoughts felt incoherent as I tried to verbalize them on the spot. On rare occasions, I mustered every ounce of courage to raise my hand and speak. So much emotional labor and time was spent working up the nerve to participate. I would agonize over this. It was time lost. The reality was that I was unprepared. To be clear, I was prepared for class by having completed the readings but I wasn't prepared with the learned skill of participation. I took cues from my peers or waited to be called on. I wanted to participate but something was in the way. I found it was not easy to be courageous and speak up. The experience of speaking up in class was stressful. It felt like there were all of these thoughts in my head that I tried to quickly organize in a way that would sound "smart." When I tried to speak it was as if a trap door would slam closed and shut all of the words inside of me. Interestingly, this was never my experience with writing. As a student, writing set my thoughts free. Speaking made my thoughts feel held captive. Now after a decade as a college professor, I am acutely aware that the challenges I faced speaking in class are faced by many college students no matter what type of institution they attend. In my classroom, I am clear on my expectations for participation. I offer strategies for how to participate, as well as an invitation to office hours to work with students facing barriers to their participation. You may not get that from every professor. You may just see on the syllabus that participation points are worth a large percentage of your final grade. You have too much on the line to let lack of participation skills be a barrier to you engaging fully in class discussion. This letter is a two-parter because I can't talk to you about participation without first talking to you about voice—your voice! When it comes to a student's voice and the ability to participate, here is my message to you: *Your voice matters in the classroom. Address your fears, disrupt your silence, and engage your voice.*

One problematic response to student silence is the idea that professors can "give student voice." It is absolutely right for professors to be responsible for thinking of the ways they should be engaging students in class discussion. And it is right for professors to create classroom spaces where students feel comfortable and safe participating in a way that is a positive experience for them. It is also right for students to be thinking about their own responsibility to foster their own voice and classroom participation. These are two interrelated yet distinct sets of responsibilities. Your voice is not for someone else to find or bestow upon you. So, do not sit around waiting for someone to invite you to speak and give you what is already yours. Here is the deal: It is on your college administration and faculty to be aware of and confront systemic and institutional inequities like racism, classism, xenophobia, sexism, and sexuality related phobias that impact student experiences and act as barriers to student participation. It is on your professor to create equitable learning spaces where students can come to voice and participate in the classroom. In some cases, students choose silence as an act of resistance to unjust educational spaces. I would never encourage a student to disrupt their silence when it is being used as a form of resistance. If your silence is not being used as a form of resistance, and is something to be worked through, then it is up to you to take control of your classroom participation by disrupting your own silence, nurturing your own voice, confronting your own fears, speaking up, and speaking out. That is not easy to do, and exhausting in spaces that don't support you. But it's absolutely necessary, so let's talk about ways for you to be supported in this journey.

I have crossed paths with many students who named being silent in the classroom. The fact that a pattern of silence existed across education contexts was telling to me. There was something far more complex happening. I began to notice that most students were often dubbed "quiet" by others, including themselves, if they didn't speak much in class. Yet are there really this many "quiet" students? How many of you reading this know a "quiet" student and think, *Really? Outside of the classroom those folks are anything but quiet!* Who has reflected on their own self and thought, *Well I may be externally quiet but if only you could hear how loud I am in my mind; if only you could see the words and thoughts roaring inside of me trying to get out.* For those students writing is often a way to get the words out. There is real value there. Yet in a classroom that means the professor is only able to learn students' thoughts and perspectives through several written assignments. However, as a student, you want to bring yourself *fully* into the classroom and that means speaking up. This raises an important question, who is a student speaking up for to begin with? Is student participation just an academic performance for the professor? For the class? Most of us have been the audience to such performances at one point or another. Or does it go beyond that? Is student participation for the collective knowledge-making of a classroom community? I truly hope so, but I know this is not always the reality. Dubbing students as "quiet" carries the risk that the "quiet" trait becomes the crutch others might depend on. Think about it, if you aren't speaking then someone else is. This crutch depends on silence and lack of voice, and reveals a classroom where the speakers are seen as the "knowers" and the non-speakers are seen as the "non-knowers." Lack of voice has little to do with who is quiet and who is outspoken. Yet that is the default that so many will fall to when making sense of it. Lack of voice often has to do with some deep seeded fears and barriers to students' participation and engagement, and ultimately the barrier to their liberation. What is needed are methods for disrupting the silence and nurturing the voice within you so that you can bring yourself authentically and fully to the classroom discussion.

Dear students, before I share with you ways to nurture and engage your voice in class so that you can speak up and speak out, I need to begin by sharing with you some thoughts on why students may not be nurturing and engaging their voices in the first place. Maybe some of these thoughts will resonate with you right away. Or maybe they will help give you the language to name your own experience so that you can figure out what work you need to do to get on your path toward class participation. So why are students so silent? And what are ways students can disrupt their silence and speak in class discussion?

(1) *Fear of Having Intellect Questioned.* When it comes down to it, everyone carries some sort of fear. Most students don't want to say something that makes them sound unintelligent. They are in a room with their professor, an expert in a specific field, and with peers who they are assuming are intelligent people as well. They are in a college classroom, a place where students are taught that so much depends on being smart. Put all of that together and speaking up comes with some pretty high stakes. Speaking up means giving people more of who you are. Speaking up means people will craft an idea of you for better or worse. To lower the risk of being seen as some sort of academic imposter, many students choose silence. If only these students knew that most of their peers struggle with this same feeling, and quite frankly most of their professors likely felt that at some point in their academic careers too. If a student does not speak then they do not give anyone an opportunity to judge them or make assumptions about them. Sounds like a safe bet, right? This strategy is one where students think their silence shields them, when in reality it can do the very opposite and work to build more barriers around them. Students' fear and silence becomes one more barrier to them being fully involved in their own learning and transformation. Their professors may think they are not invested in the class. Their grades will likely be lower as a result. Please trust me on this, when I see a student doing the *work* of processing material, questioning material, thinking critically about the material, and developing *their* expertise on the material, then I see a student who is actively engaged in their learning. When I see a student who is always silent, then I see a student who is struggling in some form and may be shielding some of their most brilliant intellect. If a student doesn't participate in discussion then I have less information about how they are understanding the material. Lack of this information means I cannot help clarify the material, or I can't help push them forward to deepen their understanding. I work to find ways to get this information from students through other methods, but you can't rely on that being the case with all professors. The student doesn't win in the situation where they choose silence. Even though they think they are saving academic face, they are actually losing valuable time, denying themselves opportunity, and compromising their own knowledge-making. So now that you know that other people have *often* felt this way, I want you to harness the energy you would have spent worrying about if you sound smart and pour that energy into disrupting the silence barrier so that you can speak in class. If you have too little experience with this and you need help, then communicate this to your professor who might have strategies for you. For example, some students like

to be the first one to raise their hand and speak because it relieves the pressure of finding the "right" moment to jump into the discussion later on. I have set up a system where I "randomly" call on some students. In fact, they are aware in advance that I am going to call on them, but the rest of the class is not. This has proved useful. After two or three times of doing this, the student most always begins participating on their own. Sometimes we all just need a lift to get us where we want to be. You might ask your professor to use that strategy. Tell them that it is hard for you to raise your hand and participate, but that you want to improve your participation. If you know you are going to be called on when discussing the reading then you can prepare in advance for that moment. The professor can help you by calling on you at a predetermined time which can alleviate the stress and anxiety that comes with finding the "perfect" moment to speak in class. We all know there is no perfect moment, there are just moments. It is up to you to make those moments work for you and your learning. Identify your needs, communicate them to your professor, and develop strategies. You will find your fears and anxiety diminish while your participation improves!

(2) *Fear of Imperfection and Missed Opportunities to Speak.* Many students are afraid of being imperfect. They fear speaking in a way that makes them sound incoherent or inarticulate. So, students will often "rehearse" in their head and when they finally get the courage to jump into the conversation the moment has passed, literally. I have witnessed this, heard about this, and experienced it myself. By the time a student feels prepared to join in, some-one else has carried the conversation forward in a new way and the student feels a moment of defeat and frustration---all of that work thinking of the perfect order of words meant that they weren't able to listen and hear the shape the conversation was taking and thereby missed the opportunities to engage. Then there are moments when professors move really fast through material. They may ask what the class thinks, and because society conditions many of us to be uncomfortable with silence, many professors will quickly seek to fill the silence by randomly calling on someone or letting a student who commonly talks in class express their opinion. With things moving so quickly, some students are up against a barrier of not having enough time to collect their ideas thoughtfully before they share them out loud. This has nothing to do with the student, and everything to do with the professor's pedagogy. Nonetheless, students often think it is a problem with them: they don't think quickly enough. They don't speak quickly enough. Somehow, they just don't "get it" like their peers do. And then they question: *How do my peers get it so*

quickly? How do my peers come up with those ideas and make those careful points so articulately? What is wrong with me? Fear of imperfection prevents students from jumping into the conversation and creates a cycle of preparing what to say, gathering the courage to say it, missing the opportunity, feeling frustrated, and landing back on square one. That is an exhausting and laborious cycle. All the while this cycle is happening, learning in the classroom is active but the student is not getting the benefits of those opportunities because they are dealing with an internal battle that no one else may be aware of. If you find yourself in that cycle, I urge you to intentionally work on breaking it.

Here is my advice to students who need to break free from that cycle: *prepare, prepare, prepare.* First, when you are reading your assigned text before class, have a notebook or laptop ready for your note taking. Organize the page by sections: (1) Key Points (2) Critical Questions (3) Important Quotes (4) Connections to Lived Experience, and (5) Ideas and Recommendations. As you read, pull out items and put them in your organized notes. Then review your organized notes before you go to class. I encourage my students to come prepared for each class by having at least one example from each of the sections prepared to share. Those students you observe speaking with confidence in your classes? Well, words might not actually just roll off their tongue, instead those students likely did a lot of behind-the-scenes work to prepare for the moment when the opportunity presented itself for them to participate in class. They did not need to think on the spot about what they should discuss and when they should do so. They had all the information prepared ahead of time, visually represented in their notes, ready to be shared through class discussion. With organization, preparation, and practice, *you* can do this too.

(3) *Fear of Having Nothing Important to Say.* Everyone wants to feel that what they say matters, and to feel that they matter. But, some students may feel that they have nothing to say that is important enough for them to voice it in class. So those students often choose silence. *How could anyone want to hear what I have to say?* they might ask themselves. *Why should I say anything if it isn't going to be earth shattering?* they wonder. *Whatever I'm thinking has already been said by someone else,* they tell themselves. Here is the deal: If you do not have anything to contribute then you need to shift your learning and engagement approach. If you are sitting in a college classroom and the material has in no way whatsoever sparked another thought, a new idea, or a critical question, then you need to ask yourself how you can engage more deeply with the material so that you can better contribute to your own learning. If you need help with that, then consider forming a study group where you discuss

the reading in advance of class so that you get a sense of how other people are engaging with the text. This will allow you to be prepared to discuss with more people in class when the time comes. Even if this study group is a party of two, that is still a useful strategy. You could also go visit your professor in office hours and challenge yourself to process the readings in that space if you are unsure about whether or not you are understanding the material. Finally, and most importantly, believe in the power of your experience as knowledge. Believe in your perspectives and your ideas. *Believe in them.* No one else will if you aren't willing to. We all have starting points. You may find yourself in the beginning stages of understanding and applying the class material. That is ok. Howeveryou engage with the material in class is valuable to you. You never know how your thoughts can help someone further their own understanding of something, and you never know how speaking your thoughts can help further your own understanding as well. But at minimum, by speaking in class you make yourself visible. Don't fear being seen. Don't fear being heard. I am not saying it will be comfortable. However, your voice is one of the most powerful tools you have. So, I am saying it will be necessary.

(4) *Shirking the Responsibility of Speaking in Class.* Coupled with feelings of not having anything important to say, some students shrug off the *responsibility* of speaking in class. As an undergraduate I felt all of these different things when it came to speaking in class, and I also did not have a sense of responsibility to participate on a regular basis. At some level I knew my grade would probably be impacted, but that was all. What I didn't consider was that by not speaking I was eschewing my responsibility and putting the burden on others to carry the weight of the labor of discussion. It was not until graduate school when I started to think about the fact that not only was my lack of participation in class unfair to me, but it was unfair to all the other people who had to speak to fill the silence. If you can sit and be silent and nothing changes for you, then you might also need to check your privilege. The classroom experience will make or break some students. Ask yourself, who are you to just sit and observe while everyone else is speaking and fighting to survive and thrive in the class? A class discussion is a weight in the college classroom and every member has a responsibility to help carry that load.

Dear students, here is the bottom line: The hope is that professors will create democratic spaces that center everyone's voice, a space where there are multiple ways to engage diverse points of view. However, not all classes are created equal, and some professors lack pedagogical knowledge to position them to create one such space. You can hope for, but not count on or wait for one such professor. So, take inventory of your class participation. Critically reflect on your fears of and barriers to speaking in class and then address them. I wish it were otherwise, but you do not have the privilege of time to wait on other people to create a perfect space for you. So, acknowledge what you are a part of and be your own advocate. Work through your fears, disrupt your silence, engage your voice, speak up and speak out. Your voice is one of your most powerful tools. Choose silence only when using it to resist spaces that exploit or oppress your voice and your experience. Otherwise, let your voice be heard.

In solidarity,
Professor Madden

Engaging your Voice "Know-How" Strategies for "Doing School"

(1) Review and activate your preparation strategies. When reading for class, create an organization section in your notes by the following headers: Key Points, Critical Questions, Important Quotes, Connections to Lived Experience, and Ideas and Recommendations. As you read, fill in these notes. Review before class. Challenge yourself to draw from these notes and share out at least once per class.

(2) Reflect on the ways you use your voice in classrooms. Is it easy, challenging, or a mix of both? What has contributed to these feelings and experiences? Taking inventory on your own participation can give you a starting point for making changes.

(3) Write down 2-3 goals for increasing using your voice in the classroom in response to each challenge. For example:

Challenge: I find the professor does not motivate me because he only uses direct lecture instruction and never pauses to interact or activate us in discussion.

Goal: Identify my learning needs to my adviser, peers, and other trusted folks on campus and get recommendations for professors who use multiple teaching methods to engage students and foster dialogue.

Challenge: The reading content in all of my major classes this semester and last were not interesting to me. I didn't read and was unable to answer questions or participate in group discussion.

Goal: Strongly reflect on if this is the right major for me since the content in all major classes didn't interest me and I didn't feel compelled to speak. Think about what topics are most interesting to me and which ones I want to talk about with others. Reevaluate my course choices and reconsider my major.

Challenge: My professor seems to favor and always call on the same students. She never calls on me. I feel like she doesn't value my voice or thoughts so I stay quiet.

Goal: I will visit office hours and communicate that I'm struggling to talk in class and it's hard for me to raise my hand. I will ask if she has strategies for me to use. I will invite her to call on me directly if I am comfortable having her do that. If she does and I soon realize that I am not comfortable being cold-called in class then I will make sure to communicate this to her. Also, I will challenge myself to speak at least once a week in class and remind myself that I cannot wait to be noticed. I am valuable without being called on and my knowledge matters. I will get noticed and speak up on my own if I am not called on. I will commit to carving out space for my own voice.

Challenge: I am in a Women's Studies class and we are only reading about the experiences of women with dominant identities like white women, able-bodied women, and middle-class women. None of this connects to my own lived experiences and I'm worried about saying the wrong thing so I don't say anything at all.

Goal: I will communicate my concerns to the professor during office hours and explain what's holding me back from participating. If I do this they might realize the importance of bringing many experiences into the classroom through a diverse and inclusive curriculum. If I am not comfortable doing this then I will seek the advice of my adviser or another trusted person on campus on how to navigate this experience of inequity in the classroom. *Please note: this is a complicated challenge because it should not be the student's responsibility to teach the professor the significance of a curriculum with multiple, diverse perspectives. This challenge to the student's participation is rooted in structural inequity and oppression. It is unfair and unjust.*

Challenge: I don't speak because I think others have more to say and my contributions aren't as important. I don't think there is value in what I have to say.

Goal: I will write down three things that I know are valuable before going to class. I will look for opportunities to connect at least one of these things during class discussion.

Goal: I will remind myself that my thoughts are valuable. My voice matters here. I will say a positive affirmation before I walk in the classroom each day such as "This moment will not happen again. Bring your voice into this moment."

Goal: I will remind myself that it is not the responsibility of others to do all the work of talking. I need to carry the labor of that work where I can. I am part of the community too.

(4) Ask yourself if your responses about using your voice in class reveal mental health challenges such as anxiety. If your responses reveal that a mental health challenge such as anxiety is impacting your participation, or even if you aren't sure but think this could be possible, then I'm sending you a warm hug and encouraging you to reach out to a trusted person and explore opportunities for professional help. First and foremost, you are not alone. Many students struggle with and work to manage anxiety disorders that impact their participation. Knowing that others manage anxiety doesn't always make us feel less alone when managing it by ourselves though. So please consider reaching out for support from someone else so that you don't have to manage this alone. If you are unsure who to connect with then you might consider the following: your campus health center where you can ask about confidential services; your resident adviser (if you live on campus); your adviser or another trusted person on campus; a supportive family member or friend. If you are looking for an off-campus starting place you might consider visiting The National Alliance on Mental Health (NAMI) website at www.nami.org which includes a phone number to talk with someone about supporting your anxiety management or other support for other mental health challenges.

(5) Remind yourself that it is a brave thing to participate. You can do hard things. Keep track of how you feel after participating. Make mental notes or jot down your feelings. Congratulate yourself on meeting your participation goals and notice how much your comfort zone grew with every class where you participated.

(6) Trust yourself.

· 6 ·

READY YOURSELF FOR YOUR BEST
PATH: PREPARE TO PARTICIPATE

Dear Students,

Many people, in many ways, have talked about the idea of luck. Perhaps at some point you have witnessed someone else's experiences and thought, "They are so lucky!" At times it seems some people have lots of luck. It's true that people get lucky in life. Though more often than not they are people who share one common thing. They are prepared. When you are prepared you are better able to claim the opportunities that life presents to you. When you are unprepared you risk missing the opportunities right before your very eyes. Don't be blind to opportunity. Don't focus on something as uncontrollable as luck. Focus on what you can control. Focus on being prepared. This letter connects to and builds intentionally on the message from Chapter 5 because now that you have thought deeply about your voice it's important you engage more discussion on preparation for participation.

Having the experience, time and space to intentionally think about and engage with methods of preparation is a privilege. Some students such as first-generation college students may not have caregivers who can share their experiences and resources on preparation for college spaces. Many people, including students, find themselves managing school with other things they are working to manage: daily life stressors, anxiety, depression, trauma, post-traumatic stress disorder, and other challenges. For others it may be having a social identity such as being an economically disadvantaged student who works multiple on or off-campus jobs to fund their education while also sending money to their family to contribute to the family income. If you identify with these things then finding the time to think about preparation could be daunting because you may be in survival mode. In this letter I focus on two key things related to preparing for participation. These are my recommended starting points for all students to establish your preparation foundation which I hope you have space to build on going forward. For now though, if you are struggling to just get through your day then these two pieces will be really crucial for you to engage as your starting points and I believe you will find them manageable. They are socio-emotional preparation for class and in-class participation preparation.

Preparing for Class

Socio-emotional Preparation

My graduate school adviser, Dr. Gretchen E. Lopez once shared something with me that I will never forget. She gave me a strategy to prepare myself for entering spaces and it goes as follows. Before doing something ask yourself, "How do I want to enter this space?" There are so many times I spent rushing through my morning going from my house to my son's school drop off only to park my car and speed walk to the classroom where I needed to teach. While I was academically prepared with my lecture to deliver, I found it important to pause for my own socio-emotional preparation as well. So, before I open the classroom door I check myself and ask "How do I want to enter this space?" On the particularly stressful mornings of balancing family and work this strategy has given me a moment to pause, check my feelings and emotions, and do a quick reset by taking a few deep breaths and slowing down my pace when I walk into the room. As a result, I find it easier to create a centered tone for the room. I am prepared to not just meet the academic needs of my students but also their socio-emotional needs. Doing this means I bring a different energy into the space with me. It is an energy that is intentional, warm, and peaceful and open to the building of awesome dynamics across the class time.

Everyone is balancing many things in their life, including you. I encourage you to think about how you enter the classroom space, or other co-curricular spaces on campus like your club meetings, team practices, service and community work, and so on. Give yourself that moment to pause and ask yourself "How do I want to enter this space?" Perhaps you are feeling anxious about going to class because you didn't sleep well or are in a bad mood about an interaction with your roommate. Pausing to check-in with how you want to enter the space can give you an opportunity to realize that you might be operating from a place of stress or lack of motivation. It could lead you to take a few deep breaths and give yourself a pep talk to center yourself and bring yourself into the space in a way that reflects how you want to be in that space: clear, focused, energized, and ready to engage. That is not saying that you should deny the range of feelings you may have prior to going into a space. This is not a call for performing like you are ok if you are not. You deserve to be authentic in all spaces. Maybe you are upset about something and it's important that you communicate it in class. Don't deny yourself your own truth. It is to say, however, that you should create a space for yourself to check-in, re-center, and prepare yourself for the new space you are heading into so that you don't deny yourself the opportunity to show up and engage in ways that reflect you living in your strength.

In-Class Participation Preparation

Did you ever stop and think about how heavily participation is weighted in your classes? Some professors choose not to assign a grade for participation. They expect that it is part of the class and that everyone should participate. Many others will assign as much as 25% of your final grade to your participation. Twenty-five percent is a lot! Here is the thing: class participation points can often make or break a student's grade, and there is debate over the fairness of this practice. What happens if you are not a talker? Should you be resigned to a lower grade for having a barrier to oral communication? The first thing you need to do is reflect on how you participate in class. What does it look like for you? This might be a brave thing to do and outside of your comfort zone, but I strongly encourage you to lean into this discomfort and communicate your participation style to your professor. Be in control of your participation. For example, a student could visit their professor early in the semester and say, "I know that class participation counts heavily in this class. I want to make sure I'm meeting your expectations for class participation. Would you tell me exactly what you are looking for and expecting from me?"

In class you will get instructions for every assignment. You will know what your professor is looking for you to do to demonstrate your understanding.

You need to also know what they are looking for with respect to class participation. Many professors don't explicitly name this and the default can be to measure participation by how much a student speaks in class. By having the conversation with your professor, you are getting the instructions for the "assignment" of class participation. This way if your professor says that participation points come down solely to speaking out loud in class you will know that you need to work on that skill. Importantly, you can also then share with your professor your own reflection on how you tend to participate in class. Discuss areas you need to address and get the guidance you need. For example, a student might say,

> I've thought about the ways I usually participate in class. It tends to look like this: I do the readings, listen carefully, and am prepared to participate by taking notes and having questions ready. But I want you to know that I really struggle with speaking up in front of the whole class. Do you have any strategies for me so I can work on this?

By naming that you have reflected on your own participation style, addressing your limitations, and asking for strategies, you have taken control over your class participation. After all, this is about you and your education. You have communicated to your professor in this conversation that you care about being prepared and you show up prepared but in ways they may not be visible to others because you have a barrier which is speaking in large groups. You further demonstrate your commitment to participation by asking for strategies to increase your readiness. Professors aren't mind readers and your communication is crucial because it sets you up early as someone who is prepared.

What happens if you challenge yourself to speak up in class, use your new strategies to do so, and still struggle with in-class participation? Then I strongly urge you to go to office hours and share with your professor in that space what you wished to share with the whole class. Take notes during class that capture the ideas and questions that arose for you during class and bring them to office hours. Name to your professor that you are still struggling to speak in class but that you want to share with them what your thoughts are and what questions arose for you. Use your meeting as a way to demonstrate your participation until you are in a place to do so in class. This practice will stretch your comfort zone when it comes to speaking about the class material with someone else and should better position you to feel more comfortable to bring those ideas and questions to the whole-class discussion. In-class participation is not easy or comfortable for many students. It is a learned practice that takes time and requires you to keep at it. The struggle with in-class participation is something that isn't often talked about. It would be helpful if professors told the class that it can be challenging and discussed this with all students early on so they know that it is a storm being weathered together, but that just doesn't seem to happen widely. As a result, the silence around this common challenge might lead you to feel that there is a stigma around finding it hard to speak up in class. Please remember, you are not alone and you can do hard things.

Talking in class can be anxiety inducing for many college students. You may be a student who works multiple jobs on campus to support yourself and your family and are too exhausted to even speak in class. Your mental health might result in challenges for you that make speaking in class and having your grades connected to speaking be especially overwhelming and stressful. If you have a 504 plan that is filed with your school's disability office then I encourage you to visit that office and communicate your concerns around grades connected to speaking in class and to also seek and use the resources available to you from that office. They will be able to support you through communicating with your professor as well. If you don't have support in place, please reach out to trusted people such as a peer, professor, coach, dean of students, resident adviser, or member of the disability office or health services office to talk through what you are managing and how it is impacting you personally and academically. There are supports available to you on campus that you might not know about, so asking a trusted person can help point you in the right direction. You deserve to have space to breathe and prepare for your experiences with intention. You deserve support in thinking about what that can look like for you and getting to a place where you are able to be an active participant in your life. You've got this.

In solidarity,
Professor Madden

Preparation for Participation "Know-How" Strategies for "Doing School"

(1) Ask yourself, "How do I want to enter this space?" before you do things. Re-center as needed so that you bring your authentic self into the space in ways that best serve you and others.
(2) Read all syllabi and identify the grade for participation.

(3) Visit office hours and ask your professor to explicitly explain what they are looking for with respect to class participation. You need to know how you will be measured.

(4) If there is no grade assigned for participation, still visit office hours and discuss class participation.

(5) Reflect and make a list of your own patterns of class participation. What do they look like? Do you complete readings so that you are prepared to talk about the text? Do you take notes while you read so that you have something to work from in class? Do you come to class with ideas and questions? Do you actively listen during class? Do you share out in partner-work? Small-group work? Whole-class discussion?

(6) Make a list of class participation areas that you need to develop.

(7) Bring your list to an office-hour meeting with your professor and consider sharing what you have learned about your own participation patterns. Ask for strategies and resources to help nurture and develop any areas of limitation. Remember, if you aren't speaking in class the professor might assume you are not an active participant. Make the invisible visible. Tell them the many ways you prepare to participate. Communicate your need for strategies to fill your participation gaps.

(8) Trust yourself.

· 7 ·

ON LISTENING

Dear Students,

Have you ever stopped and noticed the emphasis and value society places on talking? Trickling down to the college classroom, you will notice an emphasis by many faculty on talking as good classroom participation. In fact, on many syllabi it counts as a grade. After 15 years of teaching, I have observed that graded participation often translates to expectations around talk. Now I am the first to say, I want voices in my classroom that make meaningful contributions! However, participation needs to be thoughtful and intentional. I have noticed that students talking does not always translate to an ability to link discussion points and build a robust dialogue. Sure, there can be a lot of talk, but is there value in what is being said? What is the reason behind the disconnect between talk and dialogue? One reason is that oftentimes people are not deeply listening to all that has been said so their contributions risk being uninformed. This is not necessarily any fault of their own. How many classrooms have you been in that have prioritized listening instead of talking? Probably not too many. What about classrooms that have had discussions on why listening matters, as well as included activities to practice and build deep listening skills? Again, probably very few. In most classrooms, who are seen as the more "engaged" students? Usually the ones who talk the most.

Engagement and participation take many shapes and listening deserves to be given full attention. It also needs to be called to action in the classroom. If your professor doesn't do that, then you should do it for yourself. Listening is a skill everyone has to learn and actively develop. I have strategies in my classes to teach my students the process of building and engaging in constructive dialogues anchored in deep listening. I will share strategies to develop your own listening skills momentarily. Remember, the starting point for learning to dialogue begins with a call for something far more important: listening. *To participate fully in the classroom and in the world, you must open your mind and body to deep listening.*

Now I know what you might be thinking. What on earth is she talking about when she says deep listening? Basically, I want you to go beyond surface level. Picture a swimming pool. The shallow end is where you learn and the surface is pretty safe, but the deep end is where you take the plunge into quite literally unknown waters. It's where you test yourself and further reward yourself. Here is the thing I urge you to do: take the plunge into deep intellectual waters by activating your ability to go deep with your listening. To do that you have to know that listening goes way beyond engaging your ears. It means engaging your whole body too. Just as your ears absorb sound that transmits and communicates things to your brain, so too does your body. Our bodies take in energy all the time that communicates particular things and we act in response. I hear a joke and I laugh. I see a child dance and I smile. I feel a cool wind across my face and my spirit comes alive. Yet sometimes deep listening is hard. I hear a hurtful comment and my stomach twists. I see an eye roll across the room and I retreat in the physical space I am holding. I hear a perspective completely different from my own and my heart beats faster as I decide how to engage a conflicting moment. In the end, deep listening leads to deep dialogue with yourself and others. Here are some ways to engage deep listening:

(1) *Listen to Nature.* You thought this was going to be only about classroom listening, didn't you? Stay with me. We can't listen in the classroom if we aren't able to listen outside of it. Let's center ourselves first. Have you ever been at a party and right away you feel your mood totally lift? Or attended a sporting event or concert and you feel elevated by the crowd's enthusiasm and positivity? Energy is real! But energy doesn't just come from people. It comes from nature too. Do not wait until you can afford that dream beach trip to answer your body's call to relax. Listen to what your body is telling you. It sends you signals all the time. Being in nature can help you connect your body to your mind and position you to hear what you need and vice-versa.

Feeling stressed? Get outside every day so that you can gather energy from nature and repair and recharge. Shortness of breath and anxiety? Something as simple as a walk can pull fresh air into your lungs. Overwhelmed by all the noise of the world on social media? Get to the nearest lawn, kick off your shoes, sit in silence and feel the earth under your feet. Listen and follow the calling and longing of your mind and body for moments of solitude and inner peace. Hearing the singing of the birds reminds you that there is life in the air. Feeling a gusty wind can stir up your soul. Walking across snow reminds us that sometimes we have to slow down and tread carefully. Shooting stars are not cliché, but a sign that there is beauty in all things, even in the endings. Nature is telling you that you are not alone. Ever. It sends a stream of messages that we are all walking along a path in a landscape that is ever changing and ever remarkable. Take pause. There is joy to be found in taking new directions and letting ourselves go.

(2) *Listen to Yourself.* I asked a friend for advice once and she sagely responded "If a friend asked you for advice on that same problem, think about what you would tell them. Then take your advice!" I thought that was brilliant advice (Thank you, Colleen Soden!) and it has guided me ever since. Many times, when we seek advice we do so looking for reinforcement of an answer that we already know or want. Has someone ever given you advice that you asked for and you found yourself annoyed by what they said? It's because you already knew what you needed. You knew what you wanted. So, going forward, listen to yourself. Trust yourself. Follow your own advice. Yes, there are ways that other people can positively guide us with their perspectives and inform us from their own experiences. I encourage you to get many diverse perspectives on things that you don't hold the answers to or aren't in a space to think clearly or comprehensively about. But remember, you know things too. You have experiences too. For the things you *do* hold the answers to, I urge you to stand in the truth of what you know. Honor yourself by listening to yourself and taking yourself and your life seriously. It's true when people say that life is not a dress rehearsal. This is it! Show up for your own life! Abandon doubt and embrace trust in the fact that deep in your bones there are answers that you know. Listen deeply to them. Learn from them. Live through them.

You also need to listen to yourself in terms of listening to your instincts by way of listening to your gut. There is a belief that the body has two brains: one in your head and one in your gut. It is important to listen to the signals from your gut. They are communicating messages to you. There is enough that you can find online about this connection. Please trust me that your instincts will rarely steer you wrong. If something doesn't feel right, it is because it most likely is not right. Tune into your body so you can make the best decisions for your life.

(3) *Listen to Other Perspectives.* When you listen to yourself you listen to every part of yourself. You listen to your brain. Imagine you hear someone say something completely opposite of what you believe. Does your brain freeze or shut down because it's a different opinion? Pay attention to this. Do you stop listening? By extension, do you stop growing? If that happens to you, and it happens to so many people, practice pushing back against that when possible. If you were training to run a marathon and you got to the point of training where your body says, "Nope! I do not believe running another mile will benefit me because 8 miles was enough," would you stop running? No, because you committed to your development, growth, and goals. It is the same with having dialogues across differences in the college classroom. Challenge the conditioning of your brain and keep it open for business even when the business of listening is hard and uncomfortable. To shut down and stop listening is to compromise moments where you can practice perspective-taking, be further informed, and further shape and develop your own perspectives and standpoints. Listen to other perspectives, be open to growing your own, and to the possibilities of a dialogue that helps someone else's perspectives grow too.

(4) *Listen to Feedback from Educators, Especially during College.* I know it is easy for ego to get in the way of improving our academic selves. The strongest academics are the ones who are open to feedback. These folks listen to what is shared. They appreciate it and apply it. Too often people see constructive criticism as plain old criticism. When you receive feedback tell yourself that it is about the work, and not about you as a person. Don't assume the person giving you the feedback thinks that you are at a deficit. Quite the opposite. It takes a lot of time as a professor to give thoughtful and in-depth feedback. If someone is giving that to you it's because they think you are an investment. They could simply grade the paper or exam, put a letter grade on the page, and be on their way. If they gave you feedback it is because they thought it would benefit you. So be open to using the feedback for your benefit. You may not agree with every point of feedback offered to you. That's ok as long as you can rationalize why your work wouldn't benefit from it. Just don't work against good feedback or you will be working against yourself and the quality of your work. You should be more concerned when people don't give you feedback, or

when they stop investing in you. If someone isn't giving you feedback, then seek it out. You can't listen to what's not told to you.

When I was a sophomore in college, I took a hard yet influential sociology class. It wasn't the content that was hard, but the expectations around writing that I found especially challenging. For one assigned paper, I wrote what I thought was a very good piece of academic writing. I submitted it and assumed I did quite well. In that class the papers were returned via the interoffice mail system. The mailboxes were clear and I remember visiting after dinner to see my paper waiting for me. I removed it and anxiously flipped through the pages to look for my grade. I was baffled to see no letter grade at all. Just comments. I stood in shock as I read the professor's remarks that the paper was "unable to be graded." Why, you ask? Because it was terrible! My words, not the professor's. He offered many comments on what needed to be done to turn the paper around and generously gave me an opportunity to take his feedback, revise, and resubmit. I was not only shocked but annoyed. I remember thinking, "Who is he to tell me my paper is unable to be graded?! My paper is excellent! I am a wonderful writer!" My ego was definitely talking there. I did think I was a strong writer because most educators had seen me as a strong writer. Suddenly I had someone who didn't think I was up to par. Let me tell you my ego was bruised. I could have avoided the opportunity to listen to the feedback of my professor. I didn't. I brought my paper to my RA and she went through the comments with me. She encouraged me to listen to his feedback and apply it. So, I did. I was going to write a better paper. I spent more time on that paper than I did many other papers in my college career. I turned it in and a few weeks later I received it back with a B letter grade, a smiley face, and more comments on how to improve my writing in the future. That professor changed my academic life. First, he did his job. In doing so, he told me the uncomfortable truth that I wasn't used to hearing. During my first year of college my writing was not that great. My ideas were good, but my writing was not college level. College writing is a learned process and I needed to hear the expectation and strategies to improve so that I could improve. A few years ago, I found that original paper in a box of college things and I reread it. Let me tell you, it was *horrible*. I had one paragraph that went on for two complete pages—TWO PAGES! I thought back to my 18 year old self who was shocked that I did not get a good grade. The professor in me reread my work and thought, wow, I had so much to learn. It was a humbling moment and as I sit here as a professor and researcher who writes for her professional living, I am so glad that I listened to the feedback of my sociology professor, applied it, and became better. Dear students, listen to the uncomfortable truths that people tell you, especially your professors. Hear what you need to do and do it! Commit yourself to developing as students and writers, and 20 years from now when you look back at your college papers I believe that you too will be humbled and grateful.

(5) *Listen to Your Ancestors.* You are where you are as a result of generations of people whose histories paved a path for you to continue on. Heavy responsibility, isn't it? Draw strength from this knowledge. Know that you did not show up to this place alone. You brought your past with you. You are a collection of ancestral moments and legacies. Just as you need to live in your own strength as you walk your path in life, you might pause to also think of living in the strength of your ancestors. If you start to feel unsure, overwhelmed or down, then take a pause and ask yourself what the legacies of your ancestors are telling you. Anxious before a meeting, presentation, exam, or interview? Bring your ancestors into the space with you. Picture them there in the room, feel their support and encouragement. Then speak for your audience but also speak for the legacy that you continue to build on your ancestry even if it's in a completely new form.

Deep listening is an action that can truly awaken you. There is something incredibly transformative that comes from deeply listening to the world around you. Yes, it is important to listen with your mind and your gut, but don't forget to listen with your heart. It will pull you in directions that might surprise you and elevate you if you let it. When we listen to our world, we begin to fully understand our world. As we understand our world, we can write ourselves into it the way that we want based on our own truths. This is listening on the edge of our comfort zones and in spaces of bravery. It is listening that gives us permission to change our mind. It is listening that allows us to embrace the unknown. It is listening that if we let it, can change our lives.

In solidarity,
Professor Madden

Listening "Know-How" Strategies for "Doing School"

(1) Prepare for your mind and body to be a vessel for deep listening by regularly being in nature. Take walks. Sit outside in the fresh air and

meditate. Gather energy from the sun, the wind, fresh air. Listen to the earth's sounds. Reset your spirit.

(2) Reflect on your listening skills. When someone says something in class are you listening? Or are you thinking of what you could be saying and miss their point? Quiet your mind and train your brain to listen for the purpose of hearing what others are offering.

(3) Listen to connect. That first class when the professor has everyone share their names and introductions is important. Listen to how people name themselves. Commit to learning the names of your peers and building intentional connections.

(4) Listen to learn. When someone says something that you disagree with, do you listen to understand their perspective and practice perspective-taking? Or do you listen to combat their perspectives through debate? Pause and listen solely to their point.

(5) Listen for the purpose of dialogue. Practice listening for the purpose of learning and adding to collective knowledge building. Suspend judgment, practice perspective-taking, and look for places that your perspectives inform a larger body of knowledge. Build on other people's perspective points by making links where you can and build the dialogue.

(6) Listen to understand by decentering yourself. Listen from a place of knowing that people's perspectives are often informed by their lived experiences and those experiences might be quite different from your own. This means that no singular perspective may be "right." That is ok! Multiple perspectives can exist in harmony.

(7) Listen to critique with an open mind and open heart. When you receive feedback on a paper that contains critiques ask yourself if you view this as negative? Retrain your brain by telling yourself critiques are positive. They are communicating your knowledge gaps in ways that position you to do better. They are the reflection of your professor's respect for you as a person who is capable of filling those gaps. They are a commitment to your growth and invitation to you to step up on the critique, address it, and leverage yourself to the next level. They address deficits but they are not meant to cause you harm even if they may be uncomfortable for you. Read them once. Let yourself feel your feelings. Come back to them later knowing they are meant to help you. Address them. Move forward.

(8) Listen to the love. When you are feeling anxious, scared, alone, unsettled or any other range of uncomfortable emotions remember to listen to the love of those around you. Bring that love into your classroom and co-curricular spaces and remember that you are the legacy of the love of family and friends, and also of your ancestors. They are so proud of you. Listen to that love and live bravely in it.

(9) Trust yourself.

· 8 ·

YES, YOU BELONG THERE: A LETTER ON BELONGING AND COMMUNITY

Dear Students,

 If there is one thing I am certain of it is that most people want to belong. Another thing I am certain of is that in college, many people feel like they don't belong. What is it that impacts our feelings of belonging? As humans, there are many things we need to survive and thrive. Belonging, the feeling and experience of being connected to something or someone, can be essential for one's ability to thrive in college. Surely everyone benefits from moments of solitude, but it is connection, community, and belonging that are going to be the things to keep a student in college. Without a sense of belonging, many students drop out, transfer to a different school, and/or experience negative impacts on their mental health and well-being. For the times you have felt, or will feel that you do not belong at your college, I urge you to know this truth: *Yes, you belong there.*

 I will not sugarcoat anything. As I write this to you, I have just come back from my college reunion. I loved William Smith College. I still love it. It is a place I hold close to my heart. Why? Because my sense of belonging was so deep at William Smith. Decades later as I attended my class reunion and walked along Seneca Lake with one of my dearest college friends, I felt that same sense of belonging run through me. As a high school senior, I toured numerous colleges. My mom still talks about how my attitude completely lifted when I toured William Smith College. My father pulled the car over to park and my mom and I hopped out and walked down the sidewalk toward campus. Within moments, I knew this was where I wanted to be. It began as a feeling deep in my bones that I belonged there. Then that feeling materialized into an actualization.

My first semester I joined the William Smith rowing team. Being a college athlete meant I had another space within the campus community where I belonged. Being a William Smith Heron felt somehow more important to me when I was with my team and my coaches. Not to mention that being on water nearly each day felt good for my soul. Classes were going well. I was making new friends. College was what I had imagined it would be. I was happy. But as the year went on, my sense of belonging at William Smith began to shift. This was around the time I started to feel like I wasn't as smart as I always thought myself to be. I had always thought of myself as a strong writer, a thought reinforced by many teachers over the years. But college writing was a whole different ball game. As I began getting Bs and Cs on my papers, I grew anxious that I no longer knew how to be an A writer. Adding to that, I found myself lacking the opportunity to meet and socialize with people outside of my college rowing team. I really liked my teammates, but being a college athlete meant being with my team all the time. 5:00 a.m. practice led into breakfast together and evening practice led to dinner together. The only other time I had free was for classes, studying, and sleep. I liked and respected my teammates very much, but I began to realize that I wanted to meet more people. That was the point that my awareness about other people on campus outside of my team started to rise. It seemed that more and more people were socializing based on similarities such as social class. I began to notice things that I was somehow blind to for most of my first year: the fancy cars, the high-end ski jackets, the references to fancy family vacations, and the use of the word summer as a verb. I noticed the way these things seemed to stratify my peers. Eventually without the built-in social safety net of my team, I wondered where I would continue to fit in and how long it would take me to find a new social group on campus.

My first year, I also experienced a disruption to my sense of belonging when someone I was very close to left college during spring term. That friendship had become so important to me and suddenly the one person I felt truly "got me" was leaving campus for good. All at once a place I felt some sort of belonging to seemed like a different college all together. I did not feel like I could stick it out there for three more years. So, I applied to transfer and went through a similar process of finding my "dream" college. But lo and behold, what I had construed to be my dream transfer school did not accept me! I was crushed. Let's be honest. I was not crushed because I wanted to go to the school so badly, in retrospect I knew nothing about the school in terms of what actually mattered: classes, faculty, extracurriculars, and opportunities. I was crushed because I wanted to go to a place where I might have a built-in friend group and could more quickly belong since a few high school friends went there. What I was left with was having to stay where I was at a place where I was beginning to feel lonely. But if I knew then what I know now it is that I *did* belong. I had always belonged. And while I felt lonely, I wasn't actually alone. Friendships and friend groups do not always form instantaneously, especially the lasting kind. That can be hard to remember when everyone around you appears to have found instant friends and friend groups, I know. Remember, some of the most valuable collections of anything are gathered intentionally and purposefully over time. Forming friendships is a process, but it can be done! It is important to never measure your ability to form friendships against others. Always remember that everyone is experiencing the same place differently. Your freshman peers on fall sports teams were likely on campus weeks before you and so when you see them in large groups on campus the first few weeks and wonder "how did they make friends so quickly?" That is why! They had a different starting point. It is not a reflection of you! Focus on you.

Belonging takes many different shapes and forms. It is brave to acknowledge feelings of not belonging, and brave to make changes in your life such as leaving a college if you do not feel supported in your belonging. But what about if you go to make the choice to change schools and the universe blocks you by sending you a rejection letter when you apply to that dream school as a transfer? What if there are other reasons like family, finances, or geography that require you to stay where you are? Well then, you should think deeply about what you need. For me, I just needed solid, not superficial friends. I needed to feel connections. The fall of sophomore year, I went back to William Smith knowing that if I wanted to belong, I needed to widen my circle and meet new people. Slowly I branched out and gathered more friends and created new memories. Before I knew it, my life was taking shape on campus. This was not an instant friend circle, in fact it took three semesters, including a semester abroad, for me to completely find my friend group. This is where I learned that you have to put yourself out there. You have to be courageous in ways that mean facing the issue head on. If I faced the issue and nothing changed then

I could think about what else was impacting my sense of belonging and get support to face that.

So, what did I do? I tried new things. I took up running. I tried rugby. I took courses in a new discipline, sociology, which would become part of my life's work. I reached out to people for help with my writing, and I got feedback that when applied made my work better. I took on more work study hours which meant spending 10 hours a week in the basement of the library assisting the college archivist. This was fascinating work—I was tasked with unearthing the stories of the college. As I learned more about William Smith's history, I felt more connected to it in the present moment. I felt proud of the school I was a part of, a women's college that graduated the first woman doctor in the United States, Dr. Elizabeth Blackwell! I explored the Finger Lakes area, a home of the U.S. Women's Rights movement, and here again felt myself connected to moments larger than me. This gave me strength. I intentionally invited people to grab lunch after class, or go for a walk into town, or study at the library, or hang out on the weekends. This was all a process. I had to get to my place of belonging by doing and by experiencing. I had to try new classes, friendships, activities, housing, to name a few. I had to see what worked for me and what didn't. I had to know what things and which people to keep close and what and who to let go of. I had to be patient. I had to trust in the process as it was happening. This was hard especially when the glossy brochure pictures I held in my mind (these were pre-internet days folks!) had images of groups that I imagined myself just falling into the pages of and "click!" instantly belonging to. What I learned was that being a William Smith student was not a universal identity, as much as the college brochure made me feel like it could be. So, when I didn't have the instant sense of belonging I assumed that I was some sort of imposter, and didn't quite belong. Here is the thing you need to know: Belonging at your college means knowing that yes, you get to claim your identity as a student at the college. You and your peers will cheer for the same teams, graduate with pride from the same institution, and 20 years later you too may attend your own reunion to celebrate your school. But within that school, within your identity as a student of whatever college you are attending, you are experiencing identity in very different ways. There may be one "brand" of your college, but there are many types of students. *That is really important to know.* There is no single way to be a student at your institution, and there is no single way of belonging. But mark my words, you *do* belong there as much as anyone else. Even when, *especially when*, you are made to feel otherwise by individuals or the institution itself.

Dear students, let's talk about being made to feel like you don't belong. Sometimes colleges do not do a good job of thinking of the ways students experience the campus culture. Sometimes the opportunities for everyone to form social bonds are limiting. Sometimes people overlook the history of the college and the legacies that have been left behind that marginalize students on campus in spaces from dorms to classrooms to social places. It's important for everyone to consider things like, what does it mean to be a student of color at a predominately white institution? What does it mean to be from a low-income household and find yourself at an elite private college? What does it mean to be a student from a rural high school thrust into an urban college setting, or a student from an urban high school thrust into a rural college setting? What does it mean when things like your sexuality, faith, or ability is not the "status quo"? What does it mean to hold an identity that is always hidden in academic disciplines? Everyone needs to think about these things because we have a shared responsibility to cultivate spaces where everyone can belong.

Every student comes with unique experiences and histories and in my opinion, the folks working at your college and your peers would do well to learn the histories and experiences of all the students on campus. I have taught at a community college in an urban setting, a large private university in an urban setting, and an elite small private college in a rural/suburban setting. The students I taught held many diverse identities. It was my job to learn who my students were so that I could understand how they were experiencing college, and so I could understand what I could do to help them experience college from a place of belonging. As a professor, this has meant intentionally building community in my classes. Community led to connection and connection led to feelings of belonging.

I strongly encourage you to build community wherever you are. Don't wait for others to build what you need, but don't be shy about telling them they need to help build too! This is not a one person job. The key though is to start where you are: your dorm floor, your first-year seminar, your team, the town or city where your college or university is located. Build community that is an "intellectual neighborhood," a term borrowed from Toni Morrison and later engaged through an intersectional and transnational feminist framework by M. Jacqui Alexander and Chandra Talpade Mohanty (1997). Think about your vision for the community you desire. Consider what would be needed to build up and build forward this community in ways that are sustainable. I love the idea of building your own "intellectual neighborhood" because it gives you the agency to envision, create, and nurture the place you want to learn and live in and the people who will be with you. Why should I build my "intellectual neighborhood" you might ask? If there is not an intellectual tradition to build on then you can create your own. I am reminded of one student at Hamilton College, Angélica Ramos, who was in the Education Studies program. Historically the program focused on a traditional teacher preparation curriculum. I envisioned and developed the program in my time at Hamilton by creating and including social justice education courses into the program. It was taking a new form. After studying education courses through a Social Justice lens, doing related research, and in firmly knowing her intellectual and personal commitments, this student created her own interdisciplinary Social Justice Education major. It was the first of its kind at Hamilton. She created her "intellectual neighborhood" and gathered experiences in a range of courses and with a range of faculty that supported her needs and kept her on her path. I hope that serves as a transformative example of the power you hold as a student to not wait for places to join or fit into, especially spaces that are limiting, but to look for and create these "neighborhoods" for yourself. There is space for your belonging and you are able to change what the space looks like to claim the education you deserve. It all starts with knowing what you desire and deserve, connecting with trusted folks on campus who will support and guide you as needed across the process, making a plan, and moving forward one step at a time so that you can thrive in a space of your own creation.

As soon as you think of yourself as a creator and not just a person trying to fit in, you take control of your experience. Don't just look for existing campus groups to join. Think of what's important to you and create it from the ground up and invite others to join you. I have seen this work time and again. From students who started writing groups, to outdoor clubs, to students who made a concerted effort to say hello to one another when crossing campus … these students built community and built their sense of belonging in the process. For students who were not in a traditionally represented group of the college, this building of community equated to building spaces to survive and thrive on campus. You belong there on that campus. If you are too "big" for them, well then, they will just have to make room because you don't have to go anywhere. If the campus doesn't do enough to support you and your belonging, I urge you to communicate your needs to your mentors, advisers, professors, and deans. These people will likely want to hear from you, and will likely want to build support for you. It's also their job to do so. From where you stand, this work of intellectual neighborhood building can change the college. Your impact will be felt not just in your life but the lives of all others who struggle to belong on campus. While you alone can't and are not responsible for fixing a campus culture, you do share the responsibility of doing the work for yourself where you can and where you are. What a transformative thing to have your work impact yourself and ultimately others. After all, belonging is not just about individual gains but collective gains of well-being and socio-emotional prosperity. And you are deserving of all of those things. Your belonging matters.

In solidarity,
Professor Madden

Belonging and Community Building "Know-How" Strategies for "Doing School"

(1) Know that the primary responsibility to create spaces of student belonging lies squarely on the institution you are attending. It is the institution's responsibility to create spaces that foster inclusion so that students can experience belonging. However, many institutions are works in progress and not all institutions create spaces of belonging. If you don't feel like you belong, please know it is likely not a result of anything you have done. It is not your fault! It could be the result of an institution that needs to do better for its students.

(2) Reflect on what it means to you to belong at the college/university. Look for where you experience belonging and identify the characteristics of those experiences that lead to your belonging. Look for where you don't experience belonging and identify the characteristics of those experiences that lead to your not belonging. Discuss these reflections with a trusted person in your life, a person who will listen and take seriously what you are saying Other peers may be experiencing or have experienced similar things. Sharing your stories might be very helpful so that you can create your own vision as well as a shared vision of what belonging should and could look like for you and others. Move forward with intention. Be gentle with yourself. Care for yourself and others.

(3) Look for opportunities to create social bonds with others. Step outside of your comfort zone and try out things that might be completely new to you. You don't have to be perfect to try something. Go to club

meetings, join the intramural sports team, accept the invitation to the comedy show, join your floor mates in cheering on the basketball game, or participate in the campus march. You never know how these might help you bond with others and grow in attachment to your location.

(4) Create opportunities to create social bonds with others. Don't wait for something to be advertised that peaks your curiosity or interest. Think about what you are curious about. Tap into your interests. Gather a few people to join you. Embrace your power to create the space of belonging for you and others on your terms!

(5) Cast a wide social net. You may fall into social groups based on who lives in your dorm, who is in your major or program, who your teammates are or who are in the clubs or organizations that you belong to. This is a great thing. Embrace it and enjoy it. Don't let it limit you though. Be open to people and experiences other than what you know. Look to make connections and build connections across groups.

(6) Reflect on your intellectual curiosities and create your "intellectual neighborhood." If your college/university lets you create your own major then you can consider doing that for yourself if the current major offerings aren't a best fit for you.

(7) Find a mentor! Mentors are different from advisers though your adviser could be the person to turn into your mentor! Your college/ university might have a peer mentoring program that you can look into as well. As you connect with folks on campus, think about who you would like to guide you across the journey and even after you graduate. Look to someone who you have been able to build trust with, who sees you as a whole person, and who shares a similar set of commitments. Most people are where they are as a result of many factors that include mentoring. Ask the person if they would consider being a mentor for you.

(8) Leave a legacy. If you look back on your higher education journey and see how you have been able to create spaces of belonging for yourself and others, be sure to share with those coming up the road behind you. They will appreciate it, and you will be leaving a legacy of what inclusion for belonging looks like that could impact many people and the institution in positive ways.

(9) Trust yourself.

Reference

Alexander, J. M., & Mohanty, C. T. (1997). *Feminist genealogies, colonial legacies, democratic futures*. Routledge.

· 9 ·

LEARNING AS A WAY TOWARD LIVING

Dear Students,

In 1952, Bernard Malamud published a book that some 30 years later would be made into a major motion film, *The Natural*. Growing up with a baseball loving father and two brothers, this film became an instant family classic. I love it for numerous reasons. First, I too love baseball. Second, I love that the film provides an anchor to my childhood and home. Third, I love the writing. I have repeatedly found myself drawn to certain scenes in the story. They resonate with me. Not long ago, I mentored a student through a very difficult moment. It was the kind of moment that disrupts a life and disrupts a dream. What would I say to ease the pain of that moment? What would I say so they would not feel helpless? Malamud's writing echoed in my mind, and I encourage you to listen for the echo of these words should you ever find your life disrupted in college, graduate school, or anywhere after or in-between: "We have two lives … The life we learn with and the life we live with after that."

College is one of those rare times in life where you may find yourself living in a bubble. This will likely be more true if you live on a residential campus. The bubble can keep the "outside world" away for some people and some campuses. Unfortunately, a lot can be lost by living in a bubble. Sometimes students do not grasp that their actions will have real time consequences. You would be hard pressed to find a professor who had never encountered students who have plagiarized, failed a class, or were expelled from school. These are the things we encounter with our students. These are disruptions that we may be faced with when mentoring students. Professors are also aware that there are disruptions that we may never know anything about that severely impact our students and disrupt their day-to-day lives all while they are expected to learn. We know that our students break up with people they have loved. We know that our students experience disappointment at the hands of other students they trusted in friendship. We know that there are losses of family members and changes of family dynamics. We know and feel the growing concern around the mental health crisis. In our classrooms we understand that students may be depressed, anxious, hungry, and dealing with substance abuse or addiction. On top of those things, we know there are a rise of social injustices on college campuses and in larger society. Our students experience racism, sexism, classism, ableism, anti-semitism, xenophobia among other violent injustices. Sometimes these are publicized and sometimes they are not. But they exist. As a professor I know that my students are learning while living very complex lives and enduring struggle. Yes, we know about many of the rarer large-scale disruptions, but we also know that micro-disruptions happen often to our students and may go unseen or unheard. We also know that there is actually nothing "micro" about these disruptions. We know all of those things disrupt our students' learning and their lives.

Dear students, the disruptions I am naming are heavy. They are raw. They are real. They hurt. Just as professors encounter students who experience these things, so too will you encounter fellow students who experience these things. You may be among them. So, if and when that time comes, listen for the echo of Malamud's lines: "We have two lives … The life we learn with and the life we live with after that." Remember that you are *learning* a life during college. You will have brought all of your lived experiences with you to campus when you start as a first-year student, and you will live with them and through them as you journey across your college days. You will build on them with moments that will fill you with so much happiness and joy. You will also build on them with moments that can come out of nowhere and disrupt. If and when the disruptions come to you or others, please do not think you have to handle it alone. You do not. You are part of a campus community. There are people all over campus whose job it will be to support you in every way, shape, and form. If you are unsure where to seek help or guidance, then ask your residential adviser, a member of student affairs, someone in the chaplaincy, or a professor. Disruptions can come from moments that feel isolating and that isolate. Remember, many people have experienced what you are experiencing, even if it doesn't feel that way, but no one has experienced it the exact way you are experiencing it. Trained professionals are on your campus to support you. Please use these resources. Then, when you or the person you know has the support in place to help navigate this disruption, please be gentle with yourself and recognize that you are in the process of something enormous. You are in the process of learning your life. You are learning the people, places, moments, ideas, and commitments that make you thrive. You are also learning the ones that hurt and disappoint you. You are learning that all of this is part of a process of living. You will learn that there is also a next chapter: "the life you live with." Yes, there is so much learning that happens while you are in college. This time is an amazing preparation for when you step off the campus as a graduate and emerge ready to live the life you have learned over your college years. On this ending note, here is my call to you. It may sound cliché, but live a life that makes you proud. To live a life that makes you proud means you have to *learn* your life in connection with integrity. Across your time in college, take pause and ask yourself how you are *learning* this college life of yours. Is this life you are *learning* preparing you for the life you are looking to *live*? Are you learning about people and friendships by stepping outside the boundaries of your dorm, your team, and your sorority and fraternity? Are you taking chances on building new relationships? Do you actively build connections with others? Do you challenge yourself by taking a diverse range of classes that foster new ideas? Do you deeply listen to others? Do you practice perspective-taking? Do you challenge biases that you or others around you hold? Do you build community? When you cause harm or hurt, do you take responsibility? Do you care for your whole self and do you care for others? Do you value things that extend beyond the superficial and material world? Do you lean into discomfort so that you can grow? You are deserving of having the best life to live with, but make a promise to yourself to do the best learning to get there.

For what it is worth, I do not believe that we only have two lives in total. I do, however, think this pattern of a life you learn with and a life you live with happens often throughout one's own life. Learning requires a certain level of releasing ourselves to the unknown waters. Like the power of water, you will first learn by the shore and gather up energy that brings you out to sea. Out in the wide open waters you will build on that energy and rise up into an awesome wave. Can you picture it? That's your wave. That's the life you have built. I am wishing you an unforgettable ride to shore.

In solidarity,
Professor Madden

Learning as a Way Toward Living "Know-How" Strategies

(1) Create a vision for the life you want to live. What are you journeying toward? Inner peace? Moments of joy? Connection with people and places? The courage to show up fully as you are? A mind and body quiet from worry? A heart open to opportunities to express and receive authentic love?

(2) Reflect on what you have learned from your life up until this point in time. Bring that reflection into conversation with your vision for the life you want to live. Ask yourself: What have been the lessons I have learned from my life? What has my life, including the disruptions, taught me about myself? What parts of those experiences do I want to carry with me and build on? What parts am I ready to release?

(3) As you journey across higher education, take regular pauses for critical self-reflection. Ask yourself: Is the life I'm living now serving me in the ways that I deserve? Is the life I'm living now helping me grow and transform?

(4) Strength check! Ask yourself: What is my strength? Am I living in my strength even if it might be messy and imperfect? Or am I living through patterns that do not serve me or the vision for the life I seek to live?

(5) Be open to experiences outside of what is familiar. Learn a life of bravery by changing patterns for how you are currently living and inviting in new people, places, and ideas.

(6) When you encounter a disruption during your journey, reach out for support. You are not alone. Ask yourself: Am I using support systems to navigate this disruption? If not, and if you don't know where to start, reach out to a trusted person for a conversation as a starting point. Remember, a disruption doesn't define a person, but your reactions and responses to the disruption can be life-changing and life-saving.

(7) Work from a growth mindset versus a fixed mindset. Keep open. Keep learning. Keep living in ways that honor your authentic self.

(8) Trust yourself.

Reference

Malamud, B. (1952). *The natural*. Farrar, Straus, and Cudahy.

· 1 0 ·

ON HOPE

Dear Students,

My alma mater, Hobart and William Smith Colleges, had a building with seven words etched into stone above the entryway: *You Are the Hope of the World*. That phrase inspired me as a college student, and it inspires me now. Yet, I know that many college students today feel a lack of hope. I am not here to just tell you to keep hope when I know how hard that is for so many students. Instead I want to share with you some thoughts on the ways you can live hope in your life.

For me a guiding principle of hope is similar to a guiding principle of love. It is actionable. It is a verb. It is an energy that must be given space to be alive. It is not merely an inspirational idea. It is an inspirational action. We must treat it as such. The more we are actionable with hope the more we realize that it is not ours to lose or find, but it is ours to nurture and sustain and live and share. It is right there within each of us and for all of us. It may be suppressed and will need to be pulled up and out of ourselves, but you are capable of that. There may be times that you feel hope is lost during your higher education journey. If and when this happens to you please remember that while you can and should look to others as examples of hope that inspire you, try not to just think of hope as being only held within someone, someplace, or something else for you to find. You already have it. It's up to you to honor the hope within you and live it from where you stand. Reveal your hope to yourself.

One way to keep hope alive in your life during college is to first think about everything as a possibility. If hope is an actionable thing then immersing ourselves in new experiences is one sure way to give it the opportunity to be tapped into, rise up, and reveal itself. If for example you hope to meet new friends and make meaningful connection then hope calls on you to say yes to people's invitations who might be outside of your friend group. If you hope to meet a significant other in school then hope calls on you to challenge ideas you might have about what that person should look like or should be like and instead realize that many different people are possibilities in your life.

For many people saying yes to new possibilities is scary. Comfort zones exist because they are just that, comfortable. Who doesn't like to feel comfortable? Our hope is activated and lives on when we are willing to expand out comfort zones. Perhaps you are feeling hopeless about landing a job after college or graduate school so you don't apply to jobs that you think are out of your reach. Hope calls on you to still apply to those jobs in spite of any fears you may have of rejection. Perhaps you really want to express your feelings to a person you are interested in but you worry that you will be too exposed, and that they will say no to your invitation to connect. Hope calls on you to be brave and ask yourself what you would do if you weren't afraid of being told no. Ask yourself this: *What would I do if rejection were not an option? Then do that thing!* Move forward in hope knowing that there absolutely is a possibility that you will receive the answer you are seeking. Look for inspiration from your ancestors to gather strength to empower you through these moments. When faced with uncomfortable moments I always think about my ancestors crossing the Atlantic Ocean with baby in tow during the Irish famine. If they could do that to create opportunities of awesome possibility for themselves and their descendants, then who am I to not be brave? Like me, you are the legacy of bravery. Your brave decisions right now will also create a legacy for people that you may never know, but who will be grateful that you let hope live by stretching your comfort zone, being brave, and moving forward no matter the outcomes.

But what if the outcome is rejection? It is no wonder that so many hopes are weighed down by fear. Rejection hurts and can linger long in our memory. While it won't make the sting of rejection easier, it is important to know that there is always something to be learned when receiving the answer you didn't want as well. Either way, you will grow. The beauty of rejection is that it creates new opportunity. Rejection is like the ocean wave that knocks you down. It can hurt to be pushed under with tremendous force. It can be disorienting. You are tied up in something that you feel powerless over. Remember, trust the process. You also know when the wave pushes you under that it is also going to pull you up again. You are part of a cycle. Rejection is only a temporary location in the cycle of braving new opportunities anchored in hope. Guess what? The hope doesn't have to go anywhere. The bravery doesn't have to go anywhere. When you emerge, those amazing things emerge with you.

A wonderful thing about hope is that it also thrives in community. We can't live this life alone. We need one another, especially in times of hopelessness. So yes, while hope is inside of you all along waiting to be revealed, there may be times when you are flat-out physically or emotionally exhausted and find there are barriers to you engaging and revealing your own hope. You don't have to do this alone. Join with others too. Make hope-based connections in your communities. Our hopes are often part of our other commitments that matter to us: for example, relationship-building in curricular and co-curricular spaces, equity and justice, and service to others.

My hope for you is that you live with hope as a guiding force in your life. I wish you bravery. I wish you growth. I also wish you joy. So much joy. I hope you find all of these things in yourself across your higher education journey. I am confident that you will. Live in your hope, trust the process, and celebrate yourself and your communities along the way. Don't forget that hope is action. Keep open to being intentionally generous and sharing what you know with others. And while it may not be etched onto a building on your campus as it was mine, you can still etch these words across your mind and heart: *You Are the Hope of the World*. You truly are.

In solidarity,
Professor Madden

Hope "Know-How" Strategies

- Keep hope alive ... that is enough.